INSIGHT POCKET GUIDE

DUBLIN

APA PUBLICATIONS
Part of the Langenscheidt Publishing Group

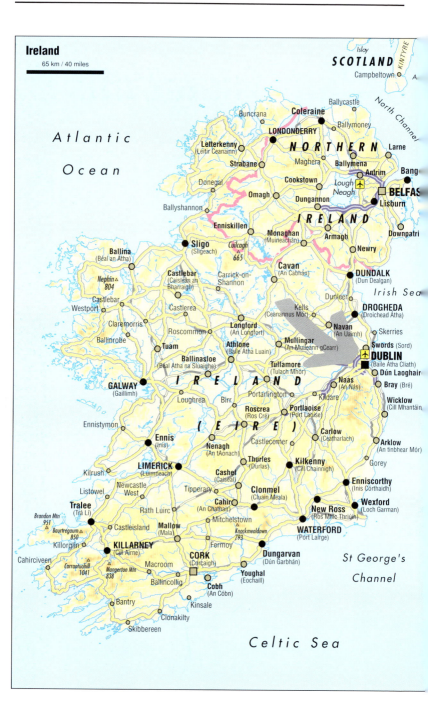

Welcome

This guidebook combines the interests and enthusiasms of two of the world's best-known information providers: Insight Guides, who have set the standard for visual travel guides since 1970, and Discovery Channel, the world's premier source of non-fiction television programming.

Its aim is to help visitors make the best use of their stay in Dublin and its surroundings in the course of seven city itineraries and five easy out-of-town excursions devised by Insight writers Donna Dailey and Mike Gerrard. The first three city tours link the essential sights – Trinity College, St Stephen's Green, the highlights of Georgian Dublin and the medieval cathedrals and castle – while four further tours explore other interesting areas and aspects of the city, from the nightlife of Temple Bar to the museums and art collections of West Dublin. The Excursions section takes in the nearby attractions of Dublin Bay, accessible on the DART railway, and samples the Wicklow Mountains, County Kildare and the Boyne Valley.

The itineraries are supported by sections on history and culture, eating out, shopping, nightlife, plus a calendar of special events and a detailed practical information section that includes a list of recommended hotels.

Donna Dailey is a travel writer and photographer who frequently writes about Ireland. She particularly enjoys the warmth and fun of Dublin, but it is more than the *craic* that keeps drawing her back. 'Because of my Irish ancestry,' she says, 'I am fascinated by Ireland's Celtic and early Christian history.'

Mike Gerrard is an award-winning travel writer whose great-great grandfather moved from Ireland to England at the time of the Great Famine. He first visited Dublin in 1992, just before a phenomenal economic boom in Ireland. He says, 'It's wonderful to compare Dublin today to the city then. It is more exciting, with excellent new museums and great food and nightlife, but it has lost none of its character or the wit and warmth of the people.'

contents

HISTORY AND CULTURE

From its Viking roots and Anglo-Norman connections to the Act of Union and the Great Famine of the mid-1800s, from the Republican fight for freedom to a new constitution in 1937, a brief account of the forces and faces that have shaped Dublin **11**

CITY ITINERARIES

These seven city itineraries link the main sights of Dublin. The first three each take a day to complete.

1 The City Centre takes a leisurely stroll between two of Dublin's most famous landmarks, Trinity College and St Stephen's Green, with opportunities to linger in some historic pubs. Includes Dublin's most famous attraction, the Book of Kells in Trinity's Old Library **21**

2 Georgian Dublin includes two of the city's elegant squares, its stately government buildings and three of Irelands's major cultural institutions – the National Gallery, the National Library and the National Museum **28**

3 Medieval Dublin takes a walk through the city's oldest streets, taking in the ancient castle and two great cathedrals, Christ Church and St Patrick's. Also includes Dublin's Viking Adventure and Dublinia, two attractions that are likely to appeal to children, and the Old Jameson Distillery and the Guinness Storehouse, devoted to two of Ireland's best-known exports **32**

4 Temple Bar is a short daytime stroll through Dublin's liveliest nightlife area for a closer look at its architectural resurrection and arts institutions. The walk, which starts at the delightful Ha'Penny Bridge, the old toll bridge, includes opportunities to buy innovative art and crafts **38**

5 North of the Liffey is a morning tour of this attractive area. The walk takes in historic buildings, several interesting off-beat museums (such as the Hot Press Irish Music Hall of Fame, the Dublin Writers' Museum and the National Wax Museum) and explores some of the city's liveliest shopping streets.. **41**

6 West Dublin is a full-day tour devoted to this historic area of the city. It visits the emotionally powerful Kilmainham Gaol, where many political prisoners were held during Ireland's struggle for independence, some wonderful art and decorative art collections, Phoenix Park and one of the finest pubs in the city **45**

7 Inner Suburbs visits several places of interest just outside the city centre including the Botanic Gardens, Glasnevin Cemetery and the birthplace of playwright George Bernard Shaw **49**

contents

EXCURSIONS

The following five excursions take in the main sights outside the city. The first two tours are short trips south and north along Dublin Bay by DART railway; excursions 3, 4 and 5 are designed as driving tours.

1 **South along Dublin Bay** is a day-long excursion to the towns south of the city, with coastal walks, castles and museums to explore and pretty scenery to enjoy along Dublin Bay..**53**

2 **North along Dublin Bay** is a day-long excursion, incorporating lovely walks from the seaside town of Howth and the 12th-century castle at Malahide **56**

3 **Around the Wicklow Mountains** looks at the stunning landscape of the Wicklow Mountains, taking in stately homes, gardens and an ancient monastic site...**59**

4 **County Kildare** involves a drive through the broad, green pastures of Kildare, heart of Ireland's horse-racing and breeding country **61**

5 **The Boyne Drive** takes you through the historic Boyne Valley, with its numerous prehistoric sites and monastic monuments, to the idyllic rolling hills and tranquil lakes of Westmeath...**63**

LEISURE ACTIVITIES

Tips on the most desirable and quirky shopping areas, the best restaurants and the liveliest night spots **67–77**

CALENDAR OF EVENTS

A guide to all the best sporting, film, music and literary festivals in Dublin...**78**

PRACTICAL INFORMATION

All the background information you are likely to need for your stay in Dublin **81**

MAPS

Ireland	4	*Temple Bar*	39
Dublin	18–19	*North of the Liffey*	41
Trinity College	22	*West Dublin*	46
City Centre	24	*Dublin Suburbs*	54
Dublin Castle	32	*Around Dublin*	58
The Old City	35	*DART and rail network*..83

CREDITS AND INDEX
pages **93–96**

Pages 2/3: Georgian doorways, Ely Place
Pages 8/9: parking outside the Temple Bar pub

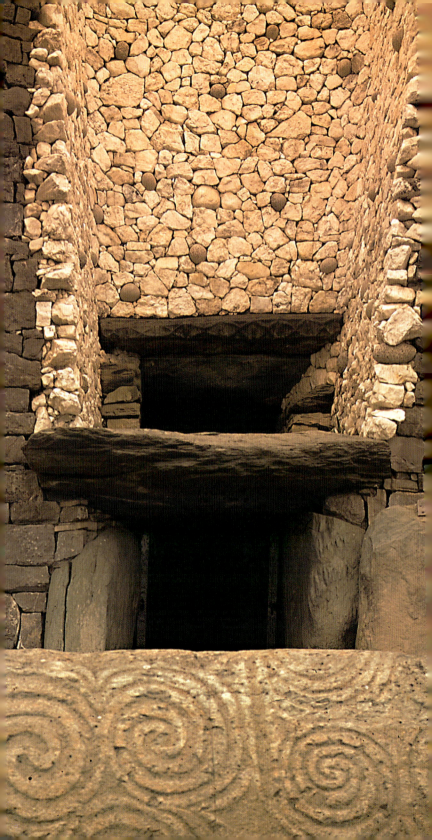

History & Culture

At the dawn of the 21st century Dublin is one of the most exciting cities in Europe, and the Irish economy is booming. No doubt the country, and its capital city, deserve this upswing in fortune. Dublin has had a particularly troubled past, and a political history that is not always easy for the outsider to follow. It is worth making the effort, however, as names such as Wolfe Tone, Michael Collins, Daniel O'Connell, Eamon de Valera and Charles Stewart Parnell recur throughout the city.

First Settlers

Mesolithic and Neolithic peoples occupied scattered settlements in the area in the 8th century BC, but it was not until the Vikings arrived in the 9th century AD that the city first put down roots. Modern Dubliners settled on 1988 as the date to celebrate their millennium: the Irish have never let fine details obstruct their ability to have a good time.

You can still see the evidence of Viking heritage in present-day Dubliners. Pale skin, blue eyes and red hair are as much Irish features as the dark hair of Celtic colleens. In the winter of 841 the Vikings settled on the banks of the Liffey, near present-day Kilmainham, before moving downstream closer to today's city centre at Wood Quay. A group of Gaelic monastic settlements already existed at a spot where the River Liffey met its tributary, the River Poddle (which is now channelled underground). A black pool formed at the point where they met, which in Irish was *dubh-linn*, the probable origin of the city's name.

Many Vikings became Christians, and mixed their raiding with trading, while establishing themselves as craftsmen, shipbuilders, carvers, jewellers and weavers. But the Norsemen also plundered Ireland, until they were defeated in 1014 by the Irish high king, Brian Boru, at the Battle of Clontarf. The established Viking communities remained and, as few Viking women came to settle here, the men intermarried with the native population.

The Anglo-Norman Invasion

It is ironic that the most notorious of Ireland's conquerors was actually invited to the country. In 1169 the exiled king of Leinster, Dermot MacMurrough, sought help from Anglo-Norman mercenaries in England in regaining his lands. The mercenaries were led by Strongbow, who married the king's daughter and set about expanding his power. The following year he conquered Dublin, and was granted a charter by the English king, Henry II. English migrants began to arrive, thus sowing the seeds of centuries of Anglo-Irish strife, which continues to devastate Northern Ireland to this day.

Left: Neolithic burial mounds at Newgrange in County Meath
Right: Tara brooch from the 8th century

history /culture

The positive side of the Anglo-Norman incursion was the flourishing of Dublin as a city. The invaders built Dublin Castle and enclosed the city within walls and towers, from the castle westwards to what is now St Augustine Street. Although few medieval buildings remain, the main east–west thoroughfare from Castle Street, continuing along Christchurch Place and High Street and beyond, still follows the route laid out by the Vikings along the ridge. Many street names, which often commemorate important patron saints, also date back to medieval times. In the 12th century the Normans also built two great city cathedrals, St Patrick's and Christ Church.

Dublin prospered, trade brought wine and exotic foods from the Mediterranean and beyond, while the land's natural fertility ensured a good supply of meat and grain. But the good life was not experienced by everyone. Though Anglo-Norman settlers in the countryside adopted Irish customs and traditions, the urban rich and powerful ensured that the native Irish were excluded from positions of authority. An area around Dublin known as the Pale marked the boundaries of English influence until Tudor times.

Of Plagues and Protestants

In the mid-14th century, rich and poor alike were wiped out by bubonic plague (commonly referred to as the Black Death), which killed roughly one Dubliner in three. Of even greater long-term significance, Henry VIII declared himself king of Ireland in 1536. Having broken away from the Church of Rome, he attempted to reverse the work of St Patrick by converting the Irish to Protestantism. Under the Reformation, Dublin's two cathedrals became part of the Church of Ireland. The great monasteries were dissolved, and Trinity College was later founded on confiscated priory land.

Many old Anglo-Irish settlers were Catholic, and they found their power displaced by the newcomers from England, whose allegiance was to London. Catholic landowners and Gaelic peasants united against injustices. In revenge for an uprising in Ulster, Oliver Cromwell's Ironside army slaughtered its way through the Irish countryside in 1649. In three years they are said to have killed around one-third of the Irish Catholic population. Despite this, Catholics remained a majority.

Above: the 9th-century *Book of Kells*
Right: Adam Loftus, first provost, Trinity College

seeds of independence

In 1685 there was a ray of hope for Ireland, when the Catholic James II succeeded his brother Charles II on the English throne. James introduced an Act of Parliament to return Irish land to its original owners, including that stolen by Cromwell's marauding army. But the English, hoping to rid themselves of the 'Popish' king, encouraged James's son-in-law, the Protestant William of Orange, to challenge him for the throne.

James travelled to Dublin and received a rousing reception from his Catholic supporters. But in July 1690, his defeat by William at the Battle of the Boyne marked a turning point in Irish history. The passions and peculiarities of politics are such that the Orangemen of Northern Ireland still march, over 300 years later, to celebrate this victory by a Dutchman over a Scotsman for the throne of England.

The Protestant victory ushered in a harsh era of discrimination against the Catholic population under severe Penal Laws. By the mid-1700s the Catholic majority owned just 7 percent of the land in Ireland.

Gradually Dublin recovered economically from the fall-out of religious conflict. Splendid new buildings began to grace the city streets, including Parliament House (now the Bank of Ireland), Mansion House, the Four Courts and the Custom House. Dublin-born Jonathan Swift became Dean of St Patrick's and set the standard for the fine literature that was to emerge from the country, with *Gulliver's Travels* and other works. Handel's *Messiah* was first performed in Dublin on 13 April 1742.

The Seeds of Independence

Irish artists and craftsmen benefited from Dublin's expansion. Furniture-makers and silversmiths proved especially gifted, while builders erected the elegant Georgian terraces around Merrion Square and St Stephen's Green. Grand country mansions like Powerscourt House and Russborough House were also built in the 18th century. Though some Catholics fared better economically, there was growing unrest at their continued suppression.

Born in Dublin in 1760, Wolfe Tone was a Protestant who believed the only way forward for Ireland was equality for all, including the persecuted Catholics. Influenced by the French Revolution, he helped to found the United Irishmen, a debating society that soon advocated armed revolt, as in the French paradigm. Indeed, French revolutionaries helped Tone fight the Irish cause, but the rebellion of 1798 failed. Tone was captured and died in prison, giving the nationalist movement its first martyr.

Fearing revolt, the British Prime Minister, William Pitt, sought to head off further trouble by proposing full union between Britain and Ireland. The Irish Parliament would be dissolved in exchange for 100 seats for Irish MPs at

Above: Jonathan Swift, who became dean of St Patrick's in 1713

Westminster. Dubliners rioted as the bill was pushed through Parliament House on College Green, largely by means of bribery and false promises of Catholic Emancipation. By appealing to persecutors and persecuted alike, the Act of Union became law on 1 January 1801.

Poets and Politicians

In the 19th century Dublin produced a prodigious crop of politicians, poets and playwrights. Ireland has given the world a disproportionate number of writers, many of them – Oscar Wilde, Bram Stoker, James Joyce, George Bernard Shaw – Dublin-born. Add such literary giants as W.B. Yeats, J.M. Synge, and talents like Samuel Beckett, Brendan Behan and Sean O'Casey and the quality of the country's literary heritage becomes apparent. Through the works of such writers, Irish culture could be expressed in the face of British oppression.

The 19th century also saw the country's inexorable progress towards freedom: in 1803, Robert Emmet attempted to seize Dublin Castle. Although he failed, he inspired a generation of revolutionaries by a speech in which he said no man should write his epitaph until 'my country takes her place among the nations of the earth'.

In 1828 Daniel O'Connell, a Catholic lawyer, campaigned for the right of Catholics to become members of parliament. He was elected to Westminster but was not allowed to take his seat because of his religion. After mass protests, the Catholic Emancipation Act was passed the next year. In 1841 O'Connell, now dubbed 'The Liberator', became the first Catholic Lord Mayor of Dublin. He campaigned for the abolition of the Act of Union, and was jailed for sedition.

O'Connell's call was taken up by younger radicals who were less committed to peaceful protest. Their cause was aided indirectly by the greatest disaster in Irish history: the failure of the potato crops in the late 1840s, which led to the Great Famine. As millions died of starvation or emigrated in desperation, the British government remained indifferent.

Charles Stewart Parnell became an MP in 1875. Although he was a Protestant landowner from Wicklow, he campaigned vigorously for Irish Home Rule, and for agrarian reform to save poor farmers from eviction. Westminster voted against the Home Rule Bill several times, and Parnell was ruined by the revelation of his affair with a married woman. In his place came wave after wave of individuals and organisations dedicated to the nationalist cause. A group calling itself the Invincibles assassinated the British Chief Secretary, Lord Cavendish, in Phoenix Park in 1882. The Irish Republican Brotherhood, forerunner of the Irish Republican Army, was also active, as were cultural organisations such as the Gaelic League, which sought to preserve the Irish language.

Above: Dublin-born author James Joyce

fight for freedom

The Fight for Freedom

Republican agitation culminated in the Easter Rising of 1916, when a group of armed nationalists, including James Connolly, seized control of buildings throughout Dublin. It took six days for British troops to quell the uprising, during which time much of the city centre was ruined. The heavy-handed British reaction turned the rebels into martyrs almost overnight. Of the 15 men who faced firing squads, Connolly was particularly badly treated, as he had already been so severely injured that he had to be tied to a chair before he could be shot.

Local response to the executions fuelled the revival of Sinn Féin ('Ourselves'). One of several late 19th-century parties dedicated to the fight for independence, Sinn Féin became a dominant force in 1917. The support enjoyed by the party became apparent in the 1918 elections, in which three-quarters of the parliamentary seats given over to Ireland were won by of Sinn Féin, even though half of its candidates were in prison. The new MPs ignored Westminster and, after declaring Ireland's independence, they set up their own parliament, the Dáil Eireann, in Dublin in January 1919. Among the MPs were two Easter Rising veterans, Eamon de Valera and Michael Collins.

The British were not prepared to give up Ireland without a fight, and the increasingly unwelcome British troops found themselves subject to the republicans' strategy of guerrilla warfare. The leading nationalist figure was Michael Collins, who had been appointed finance minister by the Dáil Eireann, though his main role was to orchestrate the killings of British soldiers and policemen.

Largely due to English and world opinion, a truce was agreed on 1 July 1921. Negotiations were put in place to create an Irish Free State comprising 26 counties, but the six counties in the northeast of Ireland, where Protestant support for the Crown was overwhelming, remained part of the United Kingdom.

The Anglo-Irish Treaty was signed in December 1921 but many, including the increasingly influential figure of Eamon de Valera, disassociated themselves from a treaty that granted only limited independence.

Civil war broke out in June 1922 and lasted for 11 months. Michael Collins was ambushed and killed when visiting his native County Cork. Many of Dublin's buildings were gutted; rebels set fire to the Public Records Office at the Four Courts, destroying historic documents, deeds and titles dating back to the 12th century.

Above: civil war erupted in 1922
Right: Michael Collins, a hero to nationalists

Having suffered under the yoke of the British, the Irish were now killing each other in their bid for freedom.

In 1926 Eamon de Valera founded Fianna Fáil (Soldiers of Destiny). By 1927, he had entered the Dáil as the head of Fianna Fáil, and by 1932 his party was in power. A new constitution was created by de Valera in 1937; he was determined to usher in independence by diplomatic rather than violent means. Newly-created Eire remained neutral during World War II, and in 1949 it left the British Commonwealth and became the Republic of Ireland.

It was as a very poor country that Ireland joined the United Nations in 1955. Many young people were still heading abroad to seek a better life, although the rate of emigration did gradually begin to slow down. Membership of the European Union (Ireland joined in 1972) brought a terrific amount of foreign investment into the country, but it took time for the benefits to become apparent. As late as the 1980s, more than one-third of Dublin's inhabitants lived below the poverty line.

The Celtic Tiger Roars

By the 1990s, the economy was starting to blossom. The arts boomed, too, not least due to the government's generous tax concessions to resident artists. Rock musicians such as Bob Geldof, U2 and Sinead O'Connor put Dublin on the world stage, and film-makers such as Neil Jordan *(The Crying Game)* and Alan Parker *(The Commitments)* contributed to a new artistic confidence. In 1991 Dublin was made European City of Culture, an honour that brought further investment into the city and which reminded the rest of Europe of Dublin's distinguished cultural heritage.

Multinational companies were attracted to Dublin by cheap property prices, tax concessions, a growing market and, in a well-educated and predominantly young population, the basis for an enthusiastic workforce. Indeed, a booming birthrate made Dublin the youngest city in Europe. By the late 1990s, the city was a fashionable weekend-break destination for Europeans.

Today Dublin is not just enjoying a return to its Georgian heyday, but surpassing it. Ireland has become known as the Celtic Tiger, and as it enters the 21st century it is truly roaring.

Above: Queen Victoria's statue is removed from the parliament building. **Left:** Dublin youth

chronology

History Highlights

7500BC First settlement of Dublin area.
2500BC Building of Newgrange passage tomb.
700BC Celts arrive in Ireland.
250BC Celts settle at mouth of River Liffey.
450AD St Patrick brings Christianity to Dublin.
841 Viking fleet winters in Dublin.
1014 Dublin's Viking king, Sitric Silkenbeard, surrenders to high king of Ireland, Brian Boru, in the Battle of Clontarf.
1038 Vikings build wooden church where Christ Church Cathedral now stands.
1170 Anglo-Normans capture Dublin.
1172 Pope confirms English king Henry II's rule over Ireland.
1191 St Patrick's Cathedral founded.
1204 Dublin Castle founded.
1347 Black Death arrives in Dublin killing one-third of the population.
1537 Henry VIII orders the dissolution of Irish monasteries.
1592 Queen Elizabeth I grants charter for founding Trinity College.
1649–52 Oliver Cromwell suppresses Ireland's Catholics.
1688 William of Orange, a Protestant Dutchman, claims English throne from King James II, a Catholic Scotsman.
1690 Battle of the Boyne. William of Orange retains throne. James flees through Dublin.
1692 Introduction of anti-Catholic Penal Laws.
1742 Première of Handel's *Messiah* in Dublin's Musick Hall.
1782 Irish Parliament secures independence from Britain.
1801 Act of Union with Britain passed, forming the United Kingdom of Great Britain and Ireland. Irish Parliament abolished.
1803 Robert Emmet, a Protestant, attempts a rebellion.
1823 Daniel O'Connell founds Catholic Association to fight for Catholics' right to become MPs.
1829 Catholic Emancipation Act.
1841 O'Connell becomes Dublin's Lord Mayor.
1843 O'Connell demands repeal of Act of Union.
1845–49 Great Famine.
1877 Parnell becomes leader of new Home Rule Party.
1881 Parnell imprisoned in Kilmainham Gaol.
1886 First Irish Home Rule Bill defeated in British Parliament.
1893 Second Home Rule Bill defeated.
1912 Third Home Rule Bill passed. Ulster Protestants threaten revolt over government from Dublin.
1916 The Easter Rising: independence from Britain and the founding of the Irish Republic proclaimed from the city's GPO building.
1919 First meeting of new Irish Parliament. De Valera elected president.
1921 Anglo-Irish Treaty; 26 counties in Ireland become the Irish Free State, but six in Northern Ireland remain part of the UK.
1922 Civil war breaks out. Michael Collins executed.
1937 New constitution. Irish Free State becomes Eire.
1949 Founding of Republic of Ireland.
1963 J.F. Kennedy, the US president, visits Dublin.
1972 Ireland joins European Union.
1974 Ulster loyalists set off bombs in central Dublin, killing 25 people.
1979 Pope John Paul II visits Dublin.
1988 Dublin celebrates its millennium.
1990 Ireland's first female president, Mary Robinson is chosen.
1991 Dublin is designated European City of Culture.
2002 Ireland joins the European Common Currency.

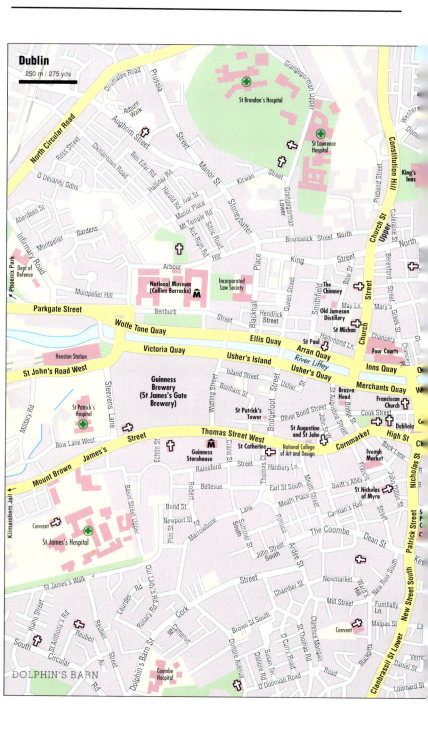

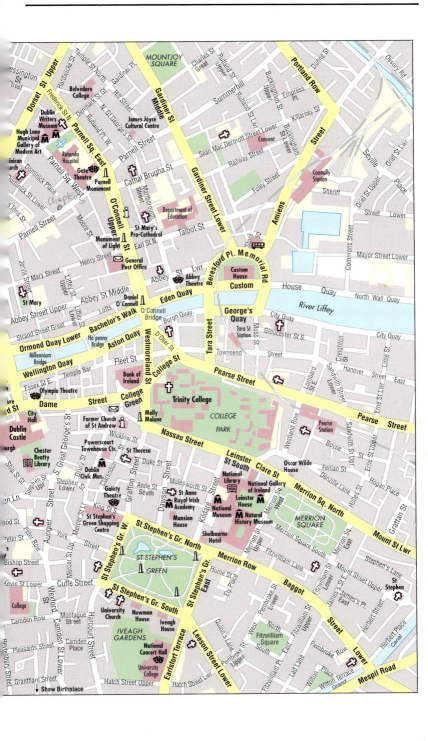

1. city centre

Orientation

Dublin sits midway along the east coast of Ireland, looking out to the Irish Sea. Although its busy suburbs stretch far to the north and south along Dublin Bay and west along the River Liffey, the main attractions are all centrally located and are easily reached on foot or by public transport. The river, which runs west to east, is Dublin's great dividing line. Apart from the area around O'Connell Street and Parnell Square, the north side is less developed, while the south side is more affluent and contains the bulk of the city's highlights. O'Connell Street and Grafton Street, joined by Westmoreland Street, form the main north–south thoroughfare, while busy main roads run east or west along the quays.

The six city itineraries are walking tours that explore Dublin's fine museums, art galleries, historic buildings and other attractions, along with the city's famous Georgian squares. Tours seven, eight and nine take you to the Botanical Gardens, Malahide Castle and other places of interest in the suburbs and along Dublin Bay, all quickly reached by bus or DART train. The final three excursions lead you into the nearby countryside to explore the beauty of the Wicklow Mountains, the Boyne Valley and County Kildare, with their monastic ruins, stately homes and gardens, prehistoric monuments and thoroughbred breeding and racing grounds. Here, a rental car and a possible overnight stay are recommended, so that you can enjoy these scenic areas at your leisure.

1. THE CITY CENTRE *(see maps, p22 & 24)*

A walk between two of Dublin's most famous landmarks, Trinity College and St Stephen's Green. Though the walk itself takes less than an hour, you could easily spend the best part of a day exploring the shops and lingering in the historic pubs.

Trinity College is a five-minute walk from the Tara Street DART station. Many city bus routes pass the college or drop you at the nearby O'Connell Bridge or adjacent quays.

The main entrance to **Trinity College**, along the West Front (facing College Green), is a popular gathering spot and an appropriate place to begin a tour of central Dublin. This, Ireland's oldest university, was founded by Queen Elizabeth I in 1592 as an attempt to steer the Irish away from 'Popery'. It remained a Protestant college until religious restrictions were lifted in 1873, but it was another century before Catholic archbishops freely allowed their flock to attend. In terms of academic prestige, Trinity ranks with England's Oxford and Cambridge universities.

Left: colonial architecture, St Stephen's Green
Right: the campanile of Trinity College

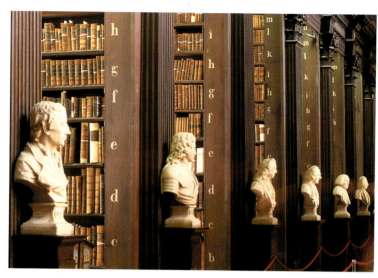

Statues of two famous alumni, the statesman Edmund Burke (1729–97) and the writer Oliver Goldsmith (1728–74) flank the entrance. Other famous past graduates include the writers Jonathan Swift, Oscar Wilde, and Samuel Beckett. Trinity's handsome architecture mostly dates from the early 18th century. The cobbled quadrangles and green squares are a world apart from the busy traffic outside the walls. Student-led tours of the campus (mid-April–Oct; fee) begin from a booth just inside the entrance every 40 minutes, starting from 10.15am (there are nine tours a day). Straight ahead is the 98-ft (30-metre) high campanile, or bell-tower, built in 1853. Other highlights include the neoclassical Examination Hall (1791) and the Venetian-style Museum Building (1857) with its domed skylights and multicoloured Irish marble pillars and staircase.

The Book of Kells

Trinity's **Old Library**, built between 1712 and 1732, houses Dublin's most famous attraction, the **Book of Kells** (open Mon–Sat 9.30am–5pm, plus Sun noon–4.30pm Oct–May and 9.30am–4.30pm Jun–Sept; admission fee). This ornately-decorated text, which contains the four gospels in Latin, is considered to be the finest illustrated medieval manuscript in the world. It was produced by scribes in the early 9th century, either at the monastery of St Columba on the Scottish island of Iona or at Kells, County Meath, to which the scribes fled from Viking raiders in AD 806; the book arrived in Trinity for safekeeping around 1653. The introductory exhibition, entitled 'Turning Darkness into Light', gives an excellent background on the creation of

Above: the Long Room, Trinity College

these medieval manuscripts, from the production of the calf-skin and inks to the symbolism of the animal motifs and intricate Celtic patterns.

After admiring the Book of Kells and other medieval works in the Treasury, head up the stairs to the **Long Room**. Its oak bookcases stretch for 213ft (65 metres) and are filled from floor to barrel-vaulted ceiling with some 200,000 of the library's oldest books. One of the few remaining copies of the 1916 Proclamation of the Irish Republic is on display, as is Ireland's oldest harp, made of willow and dating from the 15th century. The harp, which is depicted on Irish coins, is an emblem of the old bardic society.

Opposite the Old Library, the modern arts block (1980) contains the **Douglas Hyde Gallery**, a venue for experimental-arts exhibitions. From late May until the end of September, you can also see **The Dublin Experience** (daily, shows hourly 10am–5pm; admission fee), an entertaining multimedia production, which lasts for 45 minutes and gives a good introduction to Dublin history.

The Bank of Ireland

Leave Trinity College by the main gate. Opposite the campus on College Green is the **Bank of Ireland** (open Mon–Fri 10am–4pm, Thurs until 5pm), which owes its grand neoclassical facade to its earlier incarnation as Ireland's Houses of Parliament. The original central section, designed by Edward Lovett Pearce, was built between 1729 and 1739, with James Gandon's east front added in 1785. Outside is a statue of the great orator, Henry Grattan (1746–1820), who declared the independence of the Irish nation in 1782. But political autonomy was short-lived. Following the failed rebellion of 1798 and the Act of Union with England in 1801, the Irish Parliament was dissolved and the building was sold to the Bank of Ireland for £40,000.

The old House of Commons rotunda, now the bank's cash hall, has been greatly altered, but the House of Lords remains intact, with a beautiful 1,233-piece chandelier hanging from the vaulted ceiling, and tapestries depicting historic battles. You can see it during banking hours, and free 45-minute tours take place on Tuesdays at 10.30am, 11.30am and 1.45pm.

The **Bank of Ireland Arts Centre**, in an adjoining building on Foster Place, has an exhibition on 'The Story of Banking' (open Tues–Fri 10am–4pm; admission fee) and is the venue for art exhibitions and lunchtime classical music recitals; most are free.

Walk south along Grafton Street. At the corner with Suffolk Street is 'the tart with the cart', as Dubliners affectionately call the bronze statue of Molly Malone. The fictional fishmonger, immortalised in a famous Dublin song, was sculpted by Jeanne Rynhart in 1988, complete with over-laden baskets of cockles and mussels.

Right: The Duke's bar has been propped up by many Dublin writers

Though **Grafton Street** is pedestrian-only from this point, it is easily Dublin's busiest thoroughfare, particularly at the weekend when it is thronged with shoppers *(see Shopping, page 67)*. The street's acoustics are particularly kind to the city's proliferation of buskers, and at any given hour you'll hear anything from electric guitar to folk duos to hopeful youngsters belting out Irish ballads *a cappella*.

Socialising spills into side streets such as Duke Street, home to two literary watering holes. Joyce's Leopold Bloom enjoyed a Gorgonzola cheese sandwich and a glass of Burgundy at **Davy Byrne's** pub *(see Page 74)*, a favourite stop for *Ulysses* fans on Bloomsday *(see page 78)*, while many writers have propped up the bar at **The Duke** *(see page 75)* nearby.

Halfway along Grafton Street on your right is a Dublin institution, **Bewley's**

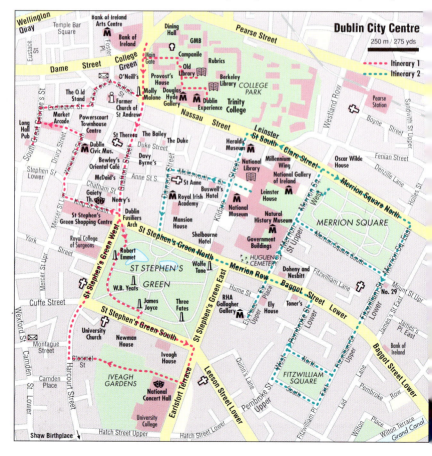

Oriental Café. A coffee or tea and cake here is as much a part of a visit to the city as a pint of Guinness. From humble beginnings as a small teashop in 1840, Bewley's became a popular meeting place and has several branches. This one, opened in 1927, retains its traditional atmosphere and has beautiful stained-glass windows by Harry Clarke. Alongside Bewley's, note the narrow passageway called Johnson's Court, a short-cut to the Powerscourt Centre *(see page 67)*. Opposite the café, Lemon Street leads to the upmarket shops of the Royal Hibernian Way *(see page 67)*.

St Stephen's Green

As you continue south on Grafton Street, look down Anne Street, on your left, for a striking view of St Anne's Church *(see page 32)*. At the end of Grafton Street, cross over the road and through the Dublin Fusiliers Arch (1904) to enter **St Stephen's Green**. One of Dublin's original commons, where public executions once took place, the 22-acre (9-ha) site was enclosed in 1663. In the late 18th century it was surrounded by elegant Georgian buildings, and the north side, a fashionable strolling place for the aristocracy, became known as Beaux Walk. With a grant from Arthur Edward Guinness, later Lord Ardilaun, in 1880, the green was laid out as it is today, with a central fountain, flower beds, a lake and a Victorian bandstand which remains a venue for lunchtime concerts in the summer.

St Stephen's Green is an irresistible spot for people-watching on a sunny day. The grounds have several fine statues, from those of patriots Robert Emmet and Countess Markievicz *(see page 26)* to Henry Moore's sculpture of the poet W. B. Yeats. Outside the railings on the northeast corner, the large monument by Edward Delaney to Wolfe Tone, leader of the 1798 rebellion, has been dubbed 'Tonehenge'. Behind it, inside the green, is a moving memorial to those who died in the Great Famine of 1845–49.

On the south side of the green at Nos 85–86 is **Newman House** (open Jun–Aug, guided tours on the hour Tues–Fri noon–5pm, Sat 2–5pm, Sun 11am–2pm; admission fee). These two houses, which were knocked together in the mid-19th century to make a home for the Catholic University of Ireland, have some of the finest interior plasterwork in the country. The house was named after its first rector, Cardinal John Henry Newman. The poet Gerard Manley Hopkins (1844–89) taught here in his last years, and his room has been preserved. James Joyce, Flann O'Brien and Eamon de Valera are among illustrious past students.

Next door is the lovely little **University Church**, with its colourful neo-Byzantine decor. Walk east past **Iveagh House** at No.

Left: Bewley's Café, a Dublin institution
Right: baroque plasterwork in Newman House

80. Built in 1730 – the first Dublin building designed by architect Richard Castle (also known as Cassels) – this later became the home of the Guinness family, and now houses the Department of Foreign Affairs. At the intersection at the southeast corner of the green, turn right and walk along Earlsfort Terrace to reach the **National Concert Hall**. Built for the Great Exhibition of 1865, it became the headquarters of University College Dublin until transformed into a concert venue in 1981.

A Lush Oasis

Nearby is one of Dublin's hidden gems. Retrace your steps, and walk through the University College car park. At the rear you will find the east entrance to **Iveagh Gardens**, a secluded pocket of lush greenery with angel statuary and fountains, and quiet benches where you can catch your breath from the city bustle. Walk through the gardens and the west entrance, turning right on Harcourt Street, which leads to the west side of St Stephen's Green. Halfway along is the **Royal College of Surgeons** which, since it opened in 1810, has played a significant role in Irish history. The bullet holes on its Doric columns are from the 1916 Easter Rising, when the nationalist rebels who occupied the building were the last to surrender. Among them was Countess Constance Markievicz, an aristocrat from Sligo, who escaped execution on account of her gender

Above: neo-Byzantine University Church
Left: Powerscourt Shopping Centre

and status. In 1918 she became the first woman elected to Westminster, but refused to take up her seat, in protest against British rule. There are more than 30,000 books in the college's library.

At the top of the green, turn left on King Street South, past the huge St Stephen's Green Shopping Centre *(see page 67)*, which covers an entire city block. Follow the street round to the right, turning right on William Street South. The former City Assembly House at No. 58 contains the small **Dublin Civic Museum** (open Tues–Sat 10am–6pm, Sun 11am–2pm; free). Among the old prints, photographs and newspaper clippings that trace Dublin's history are unusual artefacts, such as the head from the Nelson's Pillar which rose above O'Connell Street until it was blown up by the IRA in 1966. Don't miss the notice of St Stephen's Green By-Laws of 1877 by the entrance, prohibiting quarrelling, fish baskets, and 'any dog which may be reasonably suspected to be in a rabid state'.

The Powerscourt Shopping Centre

The much grander **Powerscourt Townhouse** (Mon–Fri 9am–6pm, Thurs until 7pm; admission fee) next door has undergone an impressive transformation. It was built in 1771–74 for Richard Wingfield, 3rd Viscount Powerscourt of Powerscourt House in Enniskerry *(see page 59)*, as a city residence.

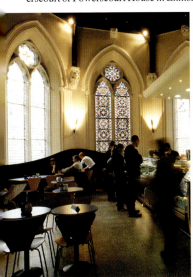

The house was sold to the government in the early 19th century, and adjoining buildings were constructed around an inner quadrangle. In 1981 it was converted into a striking shopping centre *(see page 67)*.

Opposite Powerscourt Centre, Castle Market leads to the **Market Arcade**, a covered market whose stalls sell a colourful variety of goods from jewellery to food and wine. At the far end it opens onto **South Great George's Street**. Cross the road and turn left to reach one of Dublin's most atmospheric Victorian pubs, the wood-and-glass **Long Hall** *(see page 75)*. Two other time-honoured watering holes are also nearby. Turn right out of the market and right again on Exchequer Street to reach **The Old Stand** *(see page 75)*, popular with rugby players and fans. From here, a left turn on St Andrew Street brings you to **O'Neill's** *(see page 75)*, a favourite hang-out for both tourists and students.

St Andrew's Church, opposite O'Neill's, now houses Dublin's **Tourism Centre** (open Sept–Jun Mon–Sat 9am–5.30pm; Jul–Aug Mon–Sat 9am–6.30pm, Sun 10.30am–3pm); staff can help with all the information you need for your holiday or short break in Dublin. A short walk along Suffolk Street brings you back to Trinity College.

Above: the Tourism Centre is housed in a converted church

2: GEORGIAN DUBLIN (see map, p24)

This walk takes in two of Dublin's elegant Georgian squares, its stately government buildings, and three of the city's major cultural institutions. Allow a full day to tour all the museums as well.

Several city-centre buses stop at Merrion Square. Pearse Street DART station is about a five-minute walk away.

Begin your walk at the childhood home of one of Ireland's great wits. The **Oscar Wilde House** at No. 1 Merrion Square, with its airy conservatory, looks as if it was grafted on to the brick terrace next door, but in fact it was the first house to be built on the square in 1762. Oscar was a baby when the Wilde family moved to this address in 1855, and he lived here for 23 years. The house is now owned by the American College, Dublin, which has restored several rooms, including Lady Wilde's Drawing Room (tours Mon, Wed, Thur 10.15am and 11.15am; admission fee).

Enter **Merrion Square** by the northwest gate, and turn left. In the corner, a jaunty sculpture of the author sits atop a rock, facing his old home. The square was laid out in 1762, and covers about 12 acres (5 ha). It's a lovely retreat, with shady paths winding through the lush perimeter, leading to a central green with colourful flower-beds. But the square's biggest attraction is outside the gates: the handsome Georgian terraces, called townhouses, that grace three sides.

Elegant Georgian Squares

Dublin is famous for its Georgian architecture, best seen around its five elegant squares: Merrion, Fitzwilliam, Parnell, Mountjoy and St Stephen's Green. Typically, these red-brick houses stand four storeys high above a basement. Their plain facades are broken by wrought-iron balconies on the first-floor windows. But the doors are their finest feature. Panelled and painted bright red, blue or yellow, framed by classical-style pillars and architraves, and crowned by peacock fanlights, they represent a simple but distinctive Dublin style.

Notice the blue plaques that mark the homes of distinguished former residents. On the south side, 'The Liberator' Daniel O'Connell lived at No. 58, and W.B. Yeats at No. 82, having previously resided at No. 52.

For a glimpse of what life was like in Merrion Square in Georgian times, visit **29 Lower Fitzwilliam Street** (open Tues–Sat 10am–5pm, Sun 2–5pm; closed for two weeks before Christmas; admission fee), on the southeast corner of the square. The house has been restored with period furnishings that reflect the lifestyle of a middle-class family in the late 18th century.

Continue along Fitzwilliam Street, the city's longest Georgian thoroughfare, whose charm was compromised in 1965 when 26 houses on the east side were knocked down to make way for Electricity Supply Board offices. It leads

Above: a laid-back Oscar Wilde in Merrion Square

2. georgian dublin

to **Fitzwilliam Square**, the smallest but best-preserved Georgian square in the city. It was also the last to be built, in 1825. The square itself is private. W.B. Yeats, who seems to have moved fairly frequently, lived at No. 42 for four years. His artist brother, Jack, lived at No. 18.

A Gallery for Modern Art

Walk around the square and back up Pembroke Street to Lower Baggot Street, and turn left. A detour left on Ely Place brings you to the **RHA Gallagher Gallery** (open Tues–Sat 11am–5pm, Thur till 8pm, Sun 2–5pm; free). This spacious, modern building is one of the largest exhibition spaces in Dublin and one of the most important venues in Ireland for modern art. The Royal Hibernian Academy of Arts (RHA) was founded in 1823, and its annual exhibition, held in spring, soon became a major event in the art world. Changing exhibitions focus on Irish and international artists.

Continuing west on Merrion Row towards St Stephen's Green, look out for the iron gates on your right which mark the small **Huguenot Cemetery**, dating from 1693. Thousands of Huguenot (Protestant) refugees fled to Ireland between 1650 and 1700 to escape religious persecution in France. Many settled in Dublin, where their skills in horticulture, the wine trade, silk weaving and other crafts contributed to the city's cultural development.

Just beyond the cemetery, opposite St Stephen's Green, is Dublin's grande dame, the **Shelbourne Hotel**, the entrance of which is flanked by two statues of Nubian princesses. Dating from 1824, the hotel has always been a place of power and prestige; the Constitution of the Irish Free State was drafted here in 1922. It remains a place to see and be seen.

Above: Georgian doors, Fitzwilliam Square
Right: modern art, RHA Gallagher Gallery

Retrace your steps and turn north on Upper Merrion Street, back towards Merrion Square. On your left the magnificent dome of the **Government Buildings** presides over the office of the Taoiseach (pronounced Tee-Shuck), Ireland's prime minister. Built in 1911 as the Royal College of Science, this was the last major building erected by the British. The Irish government took over the north wing in 1922, and the entire building in 1989. You can see the Cabinet Room, the Ceremonial Staircase and other highlights on a 40-minute guided tour (Sat 10.30am–12.30pm and 1.30–4.30pm; free, tickets available from the National Gallery).

Next door the **Natural History Museum** (open Tues–Sat 10am–5pm, Sun 2–5pm; free) is a wonderfully old-fashioned, Victorian place. The explorer David Livingstone gave the opening lecture in 1857. It's worth a stop just to see the wealth of taxidermy, much of it seemingly unchanged since then. Looming inside the entrance are the skeletons of three Giant Irish Deer, whose enormous antlers measure up to 13ft (4 metres). Behind them are hundreds of species of birds, fish and mammals, while upstairs a collection of world animals ranges from grizzly bears to elephants.

Continue north, past the rear side of Leinster House, to the **National Gallery** (open Mon–Sat 9.30am–5.30pm, Thur till 8.30pm, Sun noon–5.30pm; free). Its collection of Irish paintings from the 17th to early 20th centuries includes works by Nathaniel Hone, Matthew James Lawless and Roderic O'Conor. The Yeats room is devoted to the works of the great poet and his family. All the major schools of European painting are also represented. Highlights from this collection include Caravaggio's *The Taking of Christ*, Picasso's *Still Life with Mandolin*, and Gainsborough's *The Cottage Girl*. The Milltown collection comprises some 200 works from Russborough House *(see page 60)*. The new Millennium Wing, with an entrance on Clare Street, opened in 2001, giving the gallery space for special exhibitions and a home for its impressive Multimedia Gallery. You can access information on artists, themes and individual works in the collection via interactive displays. There are free guided tours of the gallery on Saturday and Sunday afternoons.

The National Library

At the top of Merrion Square, turn left on Clare Street and left again on Kildare Street. Just past the Heraldic Museum, with its banners, shields and coats of arms, is the **National Library** (open Mon–Wed 10am–9pm, Thur–Fri 10am–5pm, Sat 10am–1pm; free). Opened in 1890, its collection comprises around six million items, from rare books and manuscripts to prints, maps and newspapers. In the foyer, with a mosaic floor and stained-glass windows depicting eminent writers, changing displays are drawn from the library's archive. You can obtain a visitor's pass to enter the grand, domed Reading

Above: schoolkids having fun at the Natural History Museum

2. georgian dublin

Room on the first floor. There is also a Genealogical Office, where you can get advice on tracing your Irish ancestors, and access computerised records.

Set back between the National Library and National Museum is **Leinster House**, where the two chambers of the Irish parliament, the Dáil and the Seanad, sit. It was designed by Richard Castle and built for the Duke of Leinster in 1745. You can tour the chambers when parliament is not in session; apply at the Kildare Street entrance.

A Range of Treasures

One of the city's highlights, the **National Museum** (open Tues–Sat 10am–5pm, Sun 2–5pm; free) displays an awesome range of Celtic treasures, from gold ornaments beautifully crafted in the Bronze Age to masterpieces of religious art. The museum, built in 1890, was designed by Sir Thomas Deane, who also created the National Library. The entrance hall is a beautiful, domed rotunda, with columns of Irish marble and a splendid mosaic floor adorned by signs of the zodiac.

The sunken central gallery on the ground floor displays a fabulous collection of ancient gold jewellery, from simple *lunulae* (crescent-shaped collars) to earrings, armbands and necklaces, all crafted with great skill. Many of the gold hoards were discovered in bogs throughout the country, where they had been buried. Around the perimeter are exhibits on prehistoric Ireland, including the Lurgan logboat, made of a hollowed oak beam and over 49ft (15 metres) long. Incorporating iron and bronze weaponry, this is the world's largest collection of Celtic artefacts.

The Treasury has several highlights from the golden age of Irish art, which blossomed with the growth of Christianity after the 5th century. Highlights among the intricately-fashioned and bejewelled treasures include the Ardagh Chalice, the Tara brooch and St Patrick's bell. Upstairs, beyond the exhibits on Viking Ireland, is a room with more religious treasures, including the Cross of Cong, a processional cross made for the king of Connacht, and said to contain a relic of the True Cross. This floor also features galleries with artefacts from ancient Egypt, and space for temporary exhibitions.

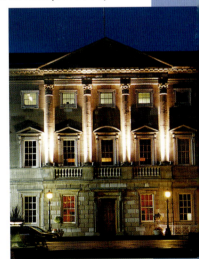

Opposite the National Museum, notice the plaque on the solicitors' office at No. 30. This was the former home of Bram Stoker, author of *Dracula*.

Above: the Reading Room of the National Library
Right: Leinster House, the seat of Parliament

Walk west on Molesworth Street, and turn left on Dawson Street. Bram Stoker, Oscar Wilde and Wolfe Tone are among those who worshipped at **St Anne's Church** (open Sun–Fri 10am–4pm). Its pretty interior was completed in 1720, and the neo-Romanesque facade was added in 1868. Near the altar is a shelf, dating from 1723, from which bread was distributed to the poor.

The Lord Mayor's Residence

Next to the church, the **Royal Irish Academy** (open Mon–Fri 9.30am–5.30pm), the country's leading academic society, houses a collection of precious Irish manuscripts. The attractive Queen Anne-style edifice set back from the street is **Mansion House**, the official residence of Dublin's Lord Mayors since 1715. It was built 10 years earlier, though the wrought-iron and stucco ornamentation are Victorian additions. The Dáil Eireann assembled here for the first time in 1919 to adopt formally the declaration of Irish independence. Today the building is mainly used for civic meetings and receptions. Turn left along St Stephen's Green to return to the Shelbourne Hotel for refreshments.

3: MEDIEVAL DUBLIN (see maps, below & p35)

A walk through the city's oldest streets, taking in the ancient castle and two great cathedrals. The walk itself takes around two hours and there are many attractions to visit, so this itinerary is best split over two days.

Dublin Castle is only a five-minute walk from Trinity College. Several buses stop along the nearby quays. Bus 123 from O'Connell Street or 78A from Aston Quay stop outside Guinness Storehouse, the furthest point.

Dublin Castle (open Mon–Fri 10am–5pm, Sat–Sun 2–5pm; admission fee) is the historic heart of the city. It stands on a ridge above the River Liffey, and its garden marks the spot of the 'black pool' (*dubh linn*) from which the city probably takes its name. Built by the Anglo-Normans in 1204, the castle was the centre of English rule in Ireland for 700 years. It was here that the British formally handed over power to Michael Collins and the Free State government in 1922.

The castle bears little resemblance to its 13th-century origins: only the stone record tower (1258) remains from medieval times. The old castle was devastated by fire in 1684, and most of the buildings date from the 18th century.

From the entrance off Dame Street walk uphill into the cobbled quadrangle of the Upper Yard, the

3. medieval dublin

city itineraries

boundary of the original castle. On your right, above the main entrance from Cork Hill, is a statue of Justice with her sword and scales, and 'her back to the nation', as Dubliners wryly observe.

You can explore the interior on a 45-minute guided tour, which leaves at regular intervals from the entrance to the State Apartments opposite. Highlights on the tour include the Grand Staircase, the Throne Room used by English monarchs, St Patrick's Hall (where Ireland's presidents are inaugurated) and the elegant drawing rooms and bedrooms, featuring beautiful plasterwork ceilings. The tour ends in the Lower Yard, where you descend to the Undercroft to see the remains of a Viking embankment and the Norman Powder Tower and moat. Across the yard is the former Chapel Royal, built in 1807–14 in Gothic style and decorated with more than 90 carved heads.

Follow the signs through the castle gardens to the **Chester Beatty Library** (open Mon–Fri 10am–5pm, Sat 11am–5pm, Sun 1–5pm; closed Mon Oct–Apr; free). You might want to spend some time here, as this collection of illustrated medieval manuscripts, Arabic texts and art treasures from the Far East, Islamic and Western worlds is truly outstanding. It was donated to the Irish nation by the American mining magnate, Sir Alfred Chester Beatty, who retired here in 1950. Among the highlights are ancient biblical papyri, with some of the earliest gospel texts, dating from the 2nd century, copies of the Koran illustrated by the great calligraphy masters, jade books from China and a range of exquisite Asian works of art from hand-painted scrolls to snuff bottles.

City Hall

Return to Dame Street for a peek at the splendid rotunda of Dublin's **City Hall** (1769–79), with its classical columns, coffered ceiling, stained-glass skylight and murals. The mosaic floor bears Dublin's coat of arms, with three defensive towers and the Latin motto 'Happy the city where citizens obey' – a sentiment not shared by the rebels who seized the building during the Easter Rising. The vaulted rooms on the lower level contain an exhibition (open Mon–Sat 10am–5.15pm, Sun 2–5pm; admission fee) on the city's history.

Cross Dame Street and head down Parliament Street towards the river. On the right is Dublin's oldest shop, Thomas Read, a cutler's established

ove: catching some rays outside Dublin Castle
ght: the rotunda and columns of City Hall

in 1670, next to a pub of the same name. Turn left on Essex Gate and right on Lower Exchange Street. On the right are the remains of Isolde's Tower, part of the 13th-century defences of the city wall, discovered during an archaeological dig in Temple Bar in 1993.

Opposite the ruins, on Essex Street West, near the heart of the original Viking settlement at Wood Quay (now covered over by the ugly blot of civic offices known as 'the bunkers'), is **Dublin's Viking Adventure** (open Tues–Sat 10am–4.30pm; Nov–Feb closed from 1–2pm; admission fee). Costumed actors provide an entertaining look at Viking life, complete with a stormy ship's journey and the sounds and smells of the recreated settlement. There is also an important collection of artefacts excavated from Wood Quay.

Walk up Fishamble Street, an ancient medieval lane. A plaque marks the site of the old Musick Hall where Handel's *Messiah* was first performed in 1742. At the top of the street is Christ Church Cathedral, but first turn right past the churchyard if you want to see **Dublinia** (open Apr–Sept daily 10am–5pm; Oct–Mar Mon–Sat 11am–4pm, Sun 10am–4.30pm; admission fee) in the former Synod Hall. A series of tableaux, of particular appeal to children, takes up the timeline from the arrival of the Anglo-Normans and Dublin's medieval history. There is also a wonderful scale model of the walled city, a multi-screen show in the Great Hall, and more artefacts from Wood Quay. A fine, covered bridge across St Michael's Hill connects the building to Christ Church, with admission on the same ticket.

Christ Church Cathedral

Built by the Vikings in about 1038, **Christ Church Cathedral** (open Mon–Fri 9.45am–5pm, Sat 9.45am–4.45pm, Sun 12.30–3.15pm; admission fee) was and is the only cathedral of Norse foundation in Ireland or Britain. It was rebuilt in Norman times, while its neo-Gothic facade and interior are the result of extensive remodelling in the 1870s. Highlights include the 15th-century brass lectern and the medieval floor tiles in the Chapel of Saint Laud, copied throughout the cathedral. The Strongbow monument is a striking effigy of the Norman leader, although the bones that lie beneath are probably not his. You can also explore the crypt, the oldest structure in Dublin, with its massive stone pillar and historic artefacts.

Nicholas and Patrick streets lead to Dublin's other great cathedral, **St Patrick's** (open Mar–Oct 9am–6pm; Nov–Feb Mon–Fri 9am–6pm, Sat 9am–5pm and Sun 10am–3pm; admission fee). St Patrick is said to have baptised converts at a well in the churchyard, and a church has stood here since the 5th century. The present cathedral was built by the Normans and restored in the mid-19th century. Highlights of the beau-

Left: Christ Church Cathedral. **Right:** St Patrick's emblem in the gardens of his cathedral

3. medieval dublin

tiful interior include the Lady Chapel, the choir and the Door of Reconciliation, through which the Earl of Kildare cut a hole and 'chanced his arm' to make peace with his enemy, the Earl of Ormond, in 1492. Jonathan Swift was dean of St Patrick's from 1713 until his death in 1745. He is buried here next to his friend Stella, and his death mask is on display. Look for the white marble bust of the blind harpist Turlough O'Carolan, the last of the great Irish bards, among the many monuments.

Ireland's First Public Library

Nearby, on St Patrick's Close, is **Marsh's Library** (open Mon and Wed–Fri 10am–12.45pm and 2–5pm, Sat 10.30am–12.45pm; admission fee). Ireland's first public library, it was built by Archbishop Narcissus Marsh in 1701. It is wonderfully atmospheric, with dark-oak bookcases and caged alcoves, where those wishing to study rare volumes were locked in. The collections contain over 25,000 books and 200 manuscripts from the 15th to 18th centuries.

St Patrick's stands in 'the Liberties' area, so called because it was outside the old city walls and thus beyond the Lord Mayor's jurisdiction. Today it is a pleasant working-class area. Walk back up Patrick Street, and cross over the road at the top of the churchyard to Hanover Lane. Turn right on John Dillon Street and look for the black iron gate halfway up on the left that leads to **St Nicholas of Myra Church** (open till noon). Built in 1829–34, it was once the city's Catholic procathedral. Its delightful interior is light and airy, with bright statues, a peach-coloured organ and a lovely blue baptistry.

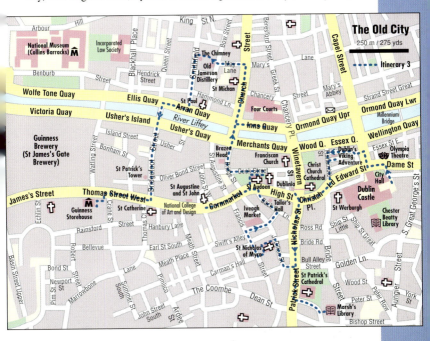

From the front entrance, turn right onto Francis Street, with its many antique shops. The **Iveagh Market Hall** was a bequest from Lord Iveagh of the Guinness family in 1907. Look for the winking stone face above the arches, said to be carved in his image. Walk along Dean Swift Square and cross Lamb Alley, turning left on Back Lane. On the right is **Tailors' Hall** (1706), Dublin's last surviving guildhall. In its heyday it played host to social and political events, and is now the headquarters of the Irish National Trust. Opposite is **Mother Redcap's Market** *(see page 67)* and a pub of the same name.

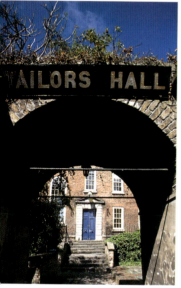

Across the High Street, two churches of **St Audoen's** stand side by side. The Catholic St Audoen's on the right was built in the mid-19th century. The Church of Ireland edifice, built in 1190, is Dublin's only remaining medieval church; its tower is thought to be the country's oldest. There is an exhibition in the guild chapel (open Jun–Sept 9.30am–5.30pm; admission fee).

St Augustine and St John

A little further west on Thomas Street is the **Church of St Augustine and St John**, designed by Edward Welby Pugin in 1872. Its 200-ft (60-metre) spire is the city's tallest, and it has a beautiful interior with a white-marble Gothic altar backed by tall stained-glass windows. Follow the steps behind the medieval church down to **St Audoen's Arch**, the last remaining gate in the old city wall, dating from 1240. Cook Street leads to Bridge Street and the Brazen Head, said to be the city's oldest pub. Ironically, it stands beside the Father Mathew Bridge, named for the founder of the 19th-century temperance crusade.

Cross the river. To the right along the quay is James Gandon's magnificent building, the **Four Courts** (built 1786–1802), which houses the High Courts. You can enter its reception area, beneath the great lantern dome, where barristers and judges congregate between court sessions.

Church Street leads to **St Michan's Church** (free; vault tours Mon–Fri 10am–12.45pm, 2–4.45pm, Sat 10am–12.45pm, admission fee), built in 1095 and named after a Danish saint. Considerably rebuilt in the late 17th century, its simple interior contains an organ on which Handel is believed to have rehearsed the *Messiah*. There is a beautiful wood-carving of 17 musical instruments, made from a single piece of oak, in front of the organ gallery.

Above: through the arch to the Tailors' Hall
Right: the Four Courts by the River Liffey

3. medieval dublin

The vaults constitute the church's most famous feature. The coffins placed here are very well preserved, due to the dry air. In one vault, the lids have fallen away to reveal mummified bodies with features such as fingernails and even heart and lungs still visible.

Turn left out of the church, and left again on May Lane, which leads to Bow Street's **Old Jameson Distillery** (open daily 9.30am–5.30pm, last tour 5pm; admission fee). Whiskey was produced here from 1780 until 1971. The craft of blending *Uisce Beatha* (the water of life), in Ireland since the 6th century, is revealed in a recreated distillery. It's an enjoyable tour, and there is a tasting at the end. The distillery shop stocks every brand of Irish Distillers Whiskey.

This area, Smithfield Village, is one of the city's oldest neighbourhoods. The Irish were moved here by the Normans, and until about a century ago it remained the city's last Gaelic-speaking redoubt. Behind Jameson's (via the twists and turns of Duck Lane) is the cobbled **Smithfield Market**, which dates back to the mid-17th century. One long-standing tradition that has resisted the neighbourhood's gentrification, is the horse and pony sale that takes place on the first Sunday of every month, amidst much lively haggling.

The Chief O'Neill hotel alongside the market typifies the new development. The hotel's bright, spacious bar is a good place for a meal or a drink. At the reception you can buy tickets to ascend **The Chimney**, an old brick tower with panoramic views over the city.

Walk back to the river and cross the bridge at Queen Street. Continue straight ahead up Bridgefoot Street and on the right you will pass **St Patrick's Tower** (*circa* 1757), the remains of the tallest smock windmill in Europe. This brick tower with a green copper dome is not open to the public, but it is a distinctive landmark.

A Stout-Drinker's Paradise

In front of **St Catherine's Church**, in Thomas Street, the patriot Robert Emmet was hanged and decapitated in 1803, following an assault on Dublin Castle. Continuing west on Thomas Street, you might pick up the scent of hops and barley wafting on the breeze as you approach the brick and stone warehouses of the Guinness brewery.

Follow the signs through this huge 55-acre (22-ha) complex, home of Dublin's most famous product, to the **Guinness Storehouse** (open Apr–Sept Mon–Sun 9.30am–6pm; Oct–Mar Mon–Sat 9.30am–5pm, Sun 10.30am–5pm; admission fee). The tour of the brewery is like no other. There are no tours of the working premises but the self-guided tour is a highly imaginative and entertaining look at all aspects of an Irish icon.

Originally built in 1904, the renovated warehouse has seven floors built

Above: Old Jameson distillery

around a central glass atrium that has been likened to a giant pint. The massive steel girders form an atmospheric backdrop to the displays. As you enter the building, notice the original 9,000-year lease on the property – signed by Arthur Guinness when he founded the brewery in 1759 – encased in the floor of the atrium. Guinness ingredients are creatively presented,

from aerated tubes of dancing hops to a gushing waterfall. On successive floors you walk through a 600-barrel copper vat and see other aspects of the brewing process, cask-making and transportation, and interesting displays of Guinness advertising campaigns. Graphic signboards give brief, informative explanations, while the soundtrack and the variety of the slick multimedia displays provide entertainment throughout the tour.

Two bars on the fifth floor serve food and drink, but for the grand finale head up to the rooftop, where you will get a complimentary pint in the Gravity Bar. The panoramic view over the city through the expansive windows constitutes one of the city's finest vistas. It's the perfect place to end your tour, relaxing with one of the 10 million glasses of Guinness that are consumed around the world every day.

4: TEMPLE BAR (see map, p39)

A short daytime stroll through Dublin's liveliest nightlife area for a closer look at its architectural resurrection and arts institutions.

Temple Bar is minutes away from O'Connell Bridge and Trinity College. All city-centre buses pass the district; the closest stops are along Wellington and Aston quays.

Temple Bar covers 28 acres (11 ha) between Dame Street and the River Liffey, with Westmoreland and Fishamble streets marking its eastern and western boundaries. It was named after Sir William Temple, who acquired the land in the early 1600s; 'bar' is an old Irish word for a riverside path. In the early 1700s Temple Bar was an area of ill repute, its narrow lanes full of pubs and prostitutes; by the middle of that century it had become a busy commercial district. The Clarence Hotel, owned by members of rock band U2, stands on the site of Dublin's original Customs House and some of the old quayside warehouses, though much altered, still remain.

Throughout the 19th century, small businesses flourished, but in the early 20th century Temple Bar, like much of central Dublin, went into decline. While the city wavered over plans to raze the area and build a new central bus depot in the 1960s, artists and small shopkeepers took out short-term leases. In the 1980s, following pressure to preserve Temple Bar, plans for the

Above: chilling out in the rooftop Gravity Bar at the Guinness Storehouse
Right: hump-backed Ha'Penny Bridge

4. temple bar

city itineraries

bus terminal were scrapped in favour of renovating it as a cultural district. Redevelopment moved into high gear when Dublin was chosen as the European City of Culture in 1991.

Today Temple Bar is the centre of Dublin's arts community: galleries, design studios, music, film and photography centres are all here. And yet, although transformed from a derelict neighbourhood into a cultural mecca, it has lost much of its bohemian character. As old buildings were converted into smart shops and flats, rents and property prices soared. The focus today is on the restaurants, pubs and nightlife. The cobbled streets and public squares are now largely the domain of teenagers and tourists. For all that, Temple Bar is one of the city's most fascinating neighbourhoods and, in its quieter hours, such as weekday mornings, the character of its old buildings shines through.

Dublin's Old Toll Bridge

Start your walk at one of Dublin's most delightful landmarks, the **Ha'Penny Bridge**. This graceful, hump-backed, cast-iron structure, erected in 1816, is a pedestrian walkway. It takes its name from the toll – a half penny – that was once charged to cross it. To the west is the Millennium Bridge, which opened in 2000 to become the fourteenth bridge across the river.

Behind the bridge is the dark passageway, **Merchants' Arch**, which leads into Temple Bar. It recalls the atmosphere of past centuries, when many streets along the quays had such archways. You emerge at **Temple Bar**

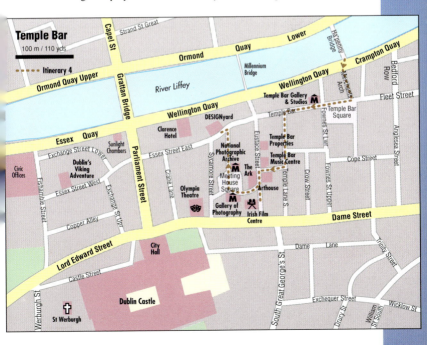

Square, which has become a lively hang-out for young people. On the northwest corner is **Temple Bar Gallery & Studios**, a former clothing factory that contains artists' studios and exhibition spaces.

Walk west on Temple Bar and turn left on Temple Lane South. On the right, a pedestrian passage known as Curved Street runs between the **Temple Bar Music Centre**, a concert venue and recording studio, and the **Arthouse** multimedia centre. Along with courses and workshops, the Arthouse displays temporary exhibitions, though not on a regular basis.

Culture at the Irish Film Centre

Curved Street leads to Eustace Street. To the right at No. 18 is **Temple Bar Properties**, where you can pick up information on cultural events and entertainment in the area. Opposite is **The Ark**, an arts centre for children *(see page 90)*. Further south, at 6 Eustace Street, is the **Irish Film Centre**, whose entrance corridor leads to a pleasant atrium with a bookshop and café. Located in a run-down building once owned by the Religious Society of Friends, this was Temple Bar's first major cultural conversion. Along with two cinemas, it houses the Irish Film Archive, a library and film production offices.

A narrow passageway beside The Ark leads into **Meeting House Square**, named after the Quaker and Presbyterian meeting houses that once opened onto it. It now serves as a superb open-air performance space during the summer. Free films are also shown, though you need to get a ticket from Temple Bar Properties in advance as numbers are limited. There is also an organic-food market on Saturday *(see page 67)*.

The square is surrounded by cultural venues, including the Gaiety School of Acting and the **Gallery of**

Above: youth culture in Temple Bar
Left: the Arthouse

5. north of the liffey

Photography (open Tues–Sat 11am–6pm, Sun 1–6pm; free) on the south side. It features changing exhibitions of international photography and has a good bookshop. On the north side, the **National Photographic Archive** (open Mon–Fri 10am–5pm, Sat 10am–2pm; free) houses the photographic collections of the National Library of Ireland and presents a series of themed exhibitions from its library of 300,000 photographs.

Iron-work gates mark the entrance to **DESIGNyard**, opposite the photographic archive. This converted warehouse is a showcase for Irish crafts. A mosaic by Sarah Daly running along the ground floor represents the River Poddle, which flows beneath the building. To the west of Parliament Street, Temple Bar contains remnants of medieval Dublin. To taste its contemporary character, wander back into the heart of the district for a drink or a meal.

5. NORTH OF THE LIFFEY *(see map below)*

A walk through this attractive area, taking in historic buildings, fine museums and busy shopping streets. Allow at least half a day if you plan to visit all the museums.

O'Connell Bridge is a five-minute walk from Tara Street DART station and the central bus station. Most city-centre buses also stop on O'Connell Street or the nearby quays.

Begin this itinerary on the north side of O'Connell Bridge (or Carlisle Bridge, as it was known when it was built in the 1790s). O'Connell Street, Dublin's main thoroughfare north of the Liffey, has monuments to Irish patriots at each end. Here, the **Daniel O'Connell monument**, unveiled in 1883, is topped by a statue of the 'uncrowned king of Ireland'. The angels around its base represent his virtues of courage, eloquence, fidelity and patriotism.

Walk up O'Connell Street and turn left along Abbey Street Middle. On the left at No. 57 is the **Hot Press Irish Music Hall of Fame** (open daily 10am–6pm; admission fee). *Hot Press* is a long-established music magazine, and this display tells the story of contemporary Irish music. Headphones guide you (not always successfully) through a series of rooms with memorabilia, music and videos of such stars as Van Morrison, U2, Rory Gallagher, Bob Geldof, the Corrs and Boyzone. When it works, it's fun and enjoyable.

Return to O'Connell Street, continue up and on your left you soon see the six unmistakable and imposing columns of the **General**

Post Office (open Mon–Sat 8am–8pm, Sun and holidays 10am–6.30pm). It was on the steps of this building on Easter Monday in 1916 that Patrick Pearse, on behalf of the rebels who had seized the buildings, read out their Proclamation of the Irish Republic. Bullet holes in the walls indicate the response of British troops. Historical connections aside, step inside to see the grand interior of the building, which evokes the scale of a Victorian railway station.

Immediately on the left after the GPO is Henry Street, with the famous **Moore Street Market** (daily 10am–6pm; *see page 67*) a short way along on the right. This flower, fruit and vegetable market is a reminder of old Dublin, with the stallholders bantering with each other and with their customers. Henry Street turns into Mary Street, both of which are mostly traffic-free. The two form one of the city's busiest shopping areas.

Statues and Monuments

Return to O'Connell Street and directly opposite on Earl Street North you will find a delightful statue of James Joyce. In the broad median of O'Connell Street, is the new Monument of Light sculpture. The top of O'Connell Street is graced by a statue of Charles Stewart Parnell topped by a liberty flame.

Parnell Square, just beyond, is one of the city's five Georgian squares.

The **Rotunda Maternity Hospital** stands on the south side of the square. Constructed in 1751–57 and designed by Richard Castle, this was the first purpose-built maternity hospital in Europe. Part of the money was raised by concerts, one of which included a recital by Franz Liszt, in the adjoining buildings. These now house a cinema and, around the corner, the renowned **Gate Theatre**. The Gate was founded in 1928 in what was originally the grand supper room of the Rotunda, with the aim of bringing foreign drama productions to Dublin. It is still going strong and is one of the city's leading theatres.

Walk up the hill along Parnell Square East to the **Garden of Remembrance** (open daily, dawn–dusk). Created in 1966, it is a peaceful spot that honours all those who sacrificed their lives in the cause of Irish freedom. At the far end of a cross-shaped pond stands Oisin Kelly's beautiful sculpture, the *Children of Lir*. According to the old Irish fable, Lir was the lord of the sea whose four children were turned into swans by his second wife. The statue movingly captures this metamorphosis.

Turn left immediately after the garden. Next to the

Above: a notice board at the Irish Music Hall of Fame
Left: the statue of James Joyce

5. north of the liffey

Abbey Presbyterian Church the **Dublin Writers' Museum** (open Mon–Sat 10am–5pm, Sun and holidays 11am–5pm, Jun–Aug till 6pm; admission fee) pays tribute to the likes of Joyce, Beckett, Shaw, Yeats and Wilde. The museum excludes living writers, and though it is a little old-fashioned compared to the city's other museums, its memorabilia includes a first edition of Bram Stoker's *Dracula*, an early, signed copy of Joyce's *Ulysses*, Brendan Behan's typewriter and Samuel Beckett's old, black, bakelite telephone, with its red button to switch off incoming calls. If in need of refreshment by now, both this and the next port of call have good cafés.

Modern Art and Waxworks

Turn right out of the museum and you will soon come to the **Hugh Lane Municipal Gallery of Modern Art** (open Tues–Thur 9.30am–6pm, Fri–Sat 9.30am–5pm, Sun and holidays 11am–5pm; free except special exhibitions). Founded in 1908 and set in the beautiful Georgian Charlemont House, the gallery has a small but interesting core collection featuring works by Monet, Degas, Renoir and Coubert, a good collection of pre-Raphaelites, and a selection of work by major Irish artists. An exciting addition is the studio of the great 20th-century Irish artist Francis Bacon, which was shipped over from London and reconstructed here. Free concerts and lectures are held in the gallery on Sunday.

Leaving the gallery, turn right, then right again at the end of the street. A short way along Granby Row you will find the **National Wax Museum** (open Mon–Sat 10am–5.30pm, Sun and holidays 12.30–5.30pm; admission fee). Here an eclectic collection ranges from famous historic figures (Wolfe Tone, James Joyce, etc) to models of the popemobile, U2 and a life-size recreation of *The Last Supper* which, it must be said, falls somewhat short of Leonardo da Vinci's original.

A detour through a rather run-down area leads to one of Dublin's grand civic edifices. On leaving the Wax Museum turn right and then left along the main road, Dorset Street. After it becomes Bolton Street, turn right up Henrietta Street to see the **King's Inns**.

It may seem improbable now, but Henrietta Street was once the address of politicians and bishops, and considered one of the most desirable places to live in Dublin. The Dublin Inns of Court at the top of the street were designed by Custom House architect James Gandon at the turn of the 19th century and are still impressive. The building is closed to the public, but you are welcome to walk around the gardens.

Right: beautiful stained glass at the Dublin Writers' Museum

Retrace your steps to the Writers' Museum and keep walking straight ahead along Denmark Street, passing on your left **Belvedere College**, the Jesuit School that James Joyce attended and which he described in *A Portrait of the Artist as a Young Man*.

Further along, Denmark Street leads into **Mountjoy Square**. The green gardens in the middle are lovely, though some of the buildings around are run down: the south side was demolished and rebuilt in the 1970s.

James Joyce Cultural Centre

Walk down the west side of Mountjoy Square, turn right when you reach Parnell Street, and right again up North Great George's Street. A short way up on the right is the **James Joyce Cultural Centre** (open Mon–Sat 9.30am–5pm, Sun and holidays 12.30–5pm; admission fee). This is a study centre, not a museum, but interested visitors are always welcome, and it is worth seeing the lovingly restored interior of this elegant, terraced Georgian townhouse.

Cross Parnell Street and walk down Marlborough Street. On your right you will pass **St Mary's Pro-Cathedral** (open daily 9.30am–5pm), the city's main Catholic church. Built in 1816–25 during anti-Catholic times, it was forced to accept a backstreet location. Its portico is copied from the Temple of Theseus in Athens and its neoclassical interior features a splendid carved altar. The Irish tenor John McCormack was a member of the esteemed Palestrina choir, which you can hear every week during the 11am Sunday Mass.

Continue along Marlborough Street to the **Abbey Theatre**. This, Ireland's national theatre, was founded in 1898 by W.B. Yeats and Lady Gregory, though the building you see before you is an unattractive 1960s replacement of the original, which burned down in 1951. Controversial productions of plays such as J. M. Synge's *The Playboy of the Western World* and Sean O'Casey's *The Plough and the Stars* were staged here, and its literary heritage continues unabated.

Walk past the theatre to the river, turning left along Eden Quay to reach the **Custom House** (open mid-Mar–Nov Mon–Fri 10am–5pm, Sat–Sun 2–5pm; Dec–mid-Mar Wed–Fri 10am–5pm, Sun 2–5pm; admission fee). Work on this architectural masterpiece was completed in 1791. It served its original purpose for only nine years, because the custom and excise office was moved to London as a result of the 1801 Act of Union. The building's colourful story is told in the Visitor Centre.

On leaving the Custom House, turn right and walk back along Eden Quay, which takes you to O'Connell Bridge.

Left: the old Custom House

6. west dublin

6: WEST DUBLIN *(see map, p46)*

Allow a full day to take in all the attractions west of the city centre, including the emotionally powerful Kilmainham Gaol, some wonderful art and decorative arts collections, Phoenix Park and one of the finest old pubs in the city.

Travel on public and tourist buses (see Getting Around, page 83). *Start at Kilmainham Gaol and work your way back towards the city centre. Local buses include the 51, 78A and 79. The Dublin Bus Tours tourist bus stops outside the Royal Hospital, a short walk from Kilmainham Gaol.*

One of the most moving experiences in the city is found at **Kilmainham Gaol** (open Apr–Sep Mon–Sat 9.30am–4pm, Sun 9am–5pm; Oct–Mar Mon–Fri 9.30am–4pm, Sun 9.30am–5pm; guided tours only; admission fee; groups must be booked at least one month in advance, tel: 453 5984).

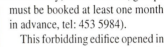

This forbidding edifice opened in 1796 and held some of the country's most notable political prisoners before it closed in 1924. The guided tour is most illuminating as it places Dublin's political history in a personal context. The hour-long tours take place at 45-minute intervals.

After watching a video about Ireland's nationalist struggle, head for the east wing, added in 1861. It was hoped that prisoners would view the skylight as the 'light of heaven' flooding down into their souls and inspiring repentance. In the chapel, Easter Rising rebels Joseph Plunkett and Grace Gifford were married on the eve of Plunkett's execution, spending just 10 minutes together as man and wife. Past the gallows is the older West Wing and the 1916 Corridor with its dark cells, where the leaders of the Easter Rising were held. Kilmainham's last prisoner, locked up during the Civil War, was Eamon de Valera, future prime minister and president of a free Ireland.

The 'Last Words'

The Irish flag flies above the Stone-breakers' Yard, where a plaque commemorates the 14 leaders of the Easter Rising who were killed here by firing squad. Before or after the tour, visit the museum which has some gruesome material, such as the display on hanging. The saddest, yet also the most heartening, exhibit is the 'Last Words', with the final letters, family photos and other memorabilia of those heroes who were put to death in 1916 in the cause of Irish independence.

On leaving the jail, turn right and walk past Kilmainham Court House, which is still in use, to **Kilmainham Gate**. Originally known as the Watling

Above: Kilmainham held some of the country's most notable political prisoners. **Right:** a plaque at the gaol

Street Gatehouse, it was moved here from Victoria Quay in 1847 in order to ease traffic congestion after the opening of the first train services to what is now Heuston Station.

Beyond the gate on the left is **Bully's Acre**, one of Dublin's oldest cemeteries, closed since the cholera epidemic of 1832. The Irish high king Brian Boru allegedly camped here before the Battle of Clontarf. The cemetery contains the remains of princes and paupers, knights and monks, as it was common ground where burial services could be performed free of charge. In the 18th and 19th centuries it was known as the haunt of body-snatchers, otherwise referred to as the 'sack-'em-up men'. They sold the cadavers from plundered graves to surgeons in Dublin and England.

The Irish Museum of Modern Art

At the end of a long and graceful approach is the **Irish Museum of Modern Art** (open Tues–Sat 10am–5.30pm, Sun and holidays noon–5.30pm; free), housed in the handsome, 17th-century Royal Hospital building. There are eight galleries spread around the various wings, with some works in the courtyard, along its colonnades, and in the Deputy Master's House nearby. The museum's own collection is enhanced by works loaned by other galleries and temporary exhibitions. Such 20th-century greats as Picasso and Modigliani are exhibited alongside Damien Hirst and Gilbert & George.

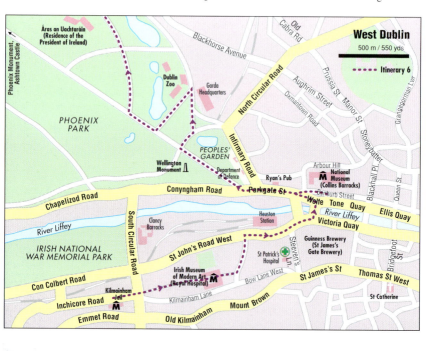

6. west dublin

The **Royal Hospital Kilmainham** was built in 1684 to house retired soldiers, the idea and buildings both modelled on Les Invalides in Paris. It remained in use until the early 20th century, when it became a Garda (police) training centre. The main hospital building is open for guided tours from June to early September (daily 10am–4.45pm; admission fee), though these hours may be extended in the future. Tours last about 45 minutes and take in the living quarters, dining hall, Great Hall and chapel. The chapel's baroque ceiling is one of the finest in Ireland; the Great Hall hosts concerts.

Decorative Arts and Phoenix Park

From outside the east entrance to the Royal Hospital, take the Dublin Bus Tours bus to the **National Museum at Collins Barracks** (open Tue–Sat 10am–5pm, Sun and holidays 2–5pm; free). This branch of the National Museum on Kildare Street houses a superb collection of decorative arts. Built as Dublin Barracks in 1701, the impressive buildings are set around the largest drill square in Europe. They were renamed in memory of Michael Collins after Irish independence. The living quarters could accommodate 5,000 soldiers; when decommissioned in 1997 they had become the oldest continuously inhabited barracks in the world.

Several splendid collections are housed on three floors in the south and west blocks of the barracks, and more rooms will open as the museum expands. The star of the show is the Curators' Choice collection, which, as the name suggests, features works selected by museum curators from around the country. There are only 25 works in this collection, but they are exquisite: check out the Dotaku Bell, a ceremonial Japanese bell from *circa* 200BC–AD250.

The Out of Storage galleries display a disparate collection of objects, uniquely arranged, with a 17th-century suit of Samurai armour next to a 1778 Gibson guitar alongside an 1825 model steam engine. Every object can be scrutinised on touch-screen computers. The collection and the computerisation are both exceptional.

Other galleries are devoted to Irish silver, scientific instruments, period furniture and Irish country furniture, as well as temporary exhibitions. The courtyard café/restaurant is run by John Cooke, of Cooke's Café fame *(see page 69)*.

Outside the barracks, turn right and walk along Parkgate Street to the wonderful **Ryan's Pub**. This is one of the finest Victorian pubs in the city, and serves tasty meals.

Turn right out of the pub towards the Park Gate entrance to **Phoenix Park**. Established in 1662 by the Duke of Ormonde, the park covers 1,700 acres (688 ha) – more than twice the size of New York's Central Park and bigger than London's three largest parks put together. You could easily

Left: *Conversation Piece* by Juan Muñoz, Irish Museum of Modern Art
Right: a leisurely stroll through Phoenix Park

spend a half-day or full day exploring it. It was the Duke of Ormonde who created a deer park here, and a herd of some 300 deer remains to this day.

To avoid the park traffic, particularly on the main thoroughfare, Chesterfield Avenue, turn right soon after the entrance where the flowerbeds of the People's Garden, dating from 1864, are still the only part of the park that is cultivated.

On the far side of Chesterfield Avenue you can see the 200-ft (63-metre) tower of **Wellington's Column**. It was begun in 1817 to commemorate the Duke of Wellington's victory at the Battle of Waterloo but was not completed for 44 years, as the duke's popularity in the city waned. He wasn't particu-

larly proud of his Irish origins: 'Being born in a stable doesn't make one a horse,' he said. Given the Dubliners' sense of mischief, it is surprising his monument wasn't moved across the way to **Dublin Zoo** *(see page 90)*. This was founded in 1830, making it the third oldest public zoo in the world.

Nearby is **Áras an Uachtaráin** (the President's Residence, closed to the public), which has been the state president's home since 1937. Built as a lodge in 1751, it was enlarged for the British viceroy. On her first visit to Ireland, Queen Victoria stayed here at the height of the famine in 1849, but her letters home make no reference to the starvation of her subjects.

The Phoenix Monument

Almost in the centre of the park is the **Phoenix Monument**, built in 1747. Near here is the source of a spring which possibly gave the park its name, *Fionne Uisce* (Clear Water in Gaelic). To the southwest is the US Ambassador's Residence, behind which lies an open space that used to be duelling grounds. The **Papal Cross** overlooks the fields and marks the spot where Pope John Paul II celebrated Mass before an estimated 1.25 million people in 1979.

If you head northwest you'll reach **Ashtown Castle**, adjacent to which is the Phoenix Park Visitor Centre (open Jun–Sep daily 10am–6pm; Oct daily 10am–5pm; Nov–mid-March Sat, Sun 9.30am–4.30pm; late March daily 9.30am–5pm; Apr–May daily 9.30am–5.30pm). The castle is a medieval tower house, and can be visited on a guided tour. The Visitor Centre tells its story, and that of Phoenix Park, while another fascinating display details the area's wildlife.

The easiest way to return to the city centre is to walk back to Dublin Zoo, where you can hop on a tour bus and head back into town.

Above: Wellington's Column in Phoenix Park
Right: Dublin Zoo

7. inner suburbs

7: INNER SUBURBS (see map, p54)

Several places of interest lie just outside the city centre, including the Botanic Gardens and the birthplace of the great Irish playwright George Bernard Shaw.

City centre buses run from O'Connell Street to the Waterways Visitor Centre and the northern sights. The Shaw Birthplace, also served by bus, is a 15-minute walk from St Stephen's Green. All sights can be reached by city centre buses.

Two attractions in the northern suburb of Glasnevin make fine retreats from the buzz of the city centre. Take bus 13 from the city centre, 19 from O'Connell Street or 134 from Middle Abbey Street to reach the **National Botanic Gardens** (open summer Mon–Sat 9am–6pm, Sun 11am–6pm; winter Mon–Sat 10am–4.30pm, Sun 11am–4.30pm; free). Founded in 1795, the gardens have some 20,000 plant species in its 48 acres (19.5 ha).

The splendid glasshouses include the Great Palm House, the Orchid House and the Curvilinear Range with varieties of rhododendrons and plants from around the world. The Alpine House shelters delicate specimens, and there are houses with ferns, cactus and succulents. Beyond the delightful rock garden, tranquil paths lead through a landscape of mature yews, conifers and a variety of hardwood species to the wall separating the grounds from Glasnevin Cemetery. Return along the border with the River Tolka, past the water-lily pond to the lovely rose garden. There is a good buffet restaurant and café, open until 5pm.

Glasnevin Cemetery

Adjoining the gardens on Finglas Road is **Glasnevin Cemetery** (take bus 13 from the city centre, 19 from O'Connell Street, or 40/40a from Parnell Street; open daily 8.30am–5pm; free). Originally called Prospect Cemetery, it opened in 1832 as a burial place for Catholics; before that date, it was

Above: one of the National Botanic Gardens' splendid glasshouses

not easy to have burials conducted according to Roman Catholics rites and procedures.

It is the country's largest graveyard, covering over 120 acres (48 ha). Over 1 million people are buried here, from 1840s famine victims to patriots such as Michael Collins, Charles Stewart Parnell, Eamon de Valera and Daniel O'Connell, who liberated Ireland from the penal laws. A fitting monument rises above his crypt, a 160-ft (49-metre) round tower built in the early Irish-Christian style. Many ornate sculptures and monuments adorn the graves, mixing Gothic and Victorian styles with carved Celtic crosses and motifs. Tours (lasting two hours) leave from the main gate at 2.30pm on Wednesday and Friday.

For a closer look at Irish sport, take bus 3, 11, 11a, 16 or 16a from the city centre, or 123 from O'Connell Street to the **GAA Museum** (open May–Sept, daily 9.30am–5pm; Oct–Apr, Tues–Sat 10am–5pm, Sun noon–5pm; admission fee) at Croke Park. The Gaelic Athletic Association (GAA) is Ireland's largest sporting organisation, and Croke Park is the home of the national games of hurling and Gaelic football. It is the venue every September of the all-Ireland championship finals in those two sports. The museum explores the history of these sports and their place in Irish culture, through historic displays, touch-screen databanks and interactive exhibits.

The Earl's Summer House

Take bus 123 from O'Connell Street, or bus 20A/20B/27/27B/42/42C from Beresford Place to reach The **Casino** at **Marino** (open May and Oct daily 10am–5pm; Jun–Sept daily 10am–6pm; Nov and Feb–Mar Sun and Thur noon–4pm; Apr Sun and Thur noon–5pm; admission fee), 3 miles (5km) north of the city centre off Malahide Road. It is said to be one of the finest Palladian buildings in Europe. The Casino is not a gambling house, but rather a summer house (*casino* means 'small house' in Italian) built for the 1st Earl of Charlemont in 1758. The house is cleverly designed, with chimneys disguised as roof urns, hollow columns that serve as drains, and a false door that gives the illusion of a single space within. The interior, in fact, contains 16 rooms,

Above and Left: Glasnevin Cemetery
Right: the Shaw Birthplace

7. inner suburbs

set around a central staircase and beautifully decorated with ornate plasterwork, silk wall hangings and marquetry flooring. Bus 42 runs on to Malahide *(see page 57)* from Marino.

East of the city centre, a 20-minute walk along Pearse Street from Trinity College brings you to the architecturally pleasing **Waterways Visitor Centre** (bus 3 from O'Connell Street also takes you there; open June–Sept daily 9.30am–5.30pm; Oct–May Wed–Sun 12.30–5.30pm; admission fee), set in the 1796 Grand Canal Basin. Although the building seems to float above the water, it has been secured on a steel and gravel base on the canal bed. In keeping with the city's penchant for coming up with pet names for any new structure, Dubliners have nicknamed the building 'the box in the docks'.

The centre tells the story of Ireland's inland waterways, built in the 18th century to provide trade and transport routes that linked Dublin with the River Shannon and the west coast. The city has two canals, the Royal Canal in the north and the Grand Canal in the south, and it is said that true Dubliners are born between them. The coming of the railways brought about the decline of the commercial era and today the canals are used for fishing and pleasure boats. There are historical exhibits in the centre, working models of engineering features and an audio-visual show.

Shaw's Birthplace

South of the centre at 33 Synge Street in the Portobello neighbourhood, a 15-minute walk from St Stephen's Green (or take bus 16/19/122 from the city centre), is the **Shaw Birthplace** (, open Easter–Oct Mon–Sat 10am–5pm, Sun 11am–5pm, closed for tours 1–2pm; admission fee). The Nobel Prize-winning playwright George Bernard Shaw was born in this house in 1856. The blue plaque on the wall simply honours him as 'author of many plays'.

Shaw had a less than happy childhood here, due to his parents' troubled marriage, but it was in this house that he began to assemble the abundance of characters that would later people his books. At the age of 20 he left for England, where he spent the rest of his life. While the house contains little from his productive years, it has been carefully restored to present a faithful picture of middle-class Victorian domestic life, with the kitchen, bedrooms, nursery and parlour all furnished in period style.

Excursions

1. SOUTH ALONG DUBLIN BAY *(see map, p54)*

The seaside towns south of the city make an easy day or half-day excursion from Dublin. There are coastal walks, castles and museums to explore, or you might prefer to just sit back and enjoy the pretty scenery along Dublin Bay.

The DART line from Dublin stops at all the towns on this itinerary, and there is also a city bus service. If you're driving, the coastal road between Dalkey and Bray gives stunning views over Killiney Bay.

The DART line south from the capital follows the path of Ireland's first rail line, which ran from Dublin's Westland Row to Dún Laoghaire, then called Kingstown, in 1834. The suburban view opens out to a large sweep of sand along Dublin Bay at **Booterstown**, where a marshland bird sanctuary manages to thrive between the railroad and the motorway.

Ireland's Main Ferry Port

Get off four stops later for **Dún Laoghaire** (pronounced *Dunleary*), Ireland's main ferry port. Its Celtic name derives from the fort *(dún)* of Laoghaire, a high king of Ireland, which stood here around the time of St Patrick. Its remains were destroyed during construction of the railway line. King George IV sailed over from England for a visit in 1821, and the town was called Kingstown in his honour for the next 100 years before reverting to its original name after Irish independence.

Though more of a suburb today, Dún Laoghaire was once a resort town and its handsome terraces and brightly painted houses retain some of their former elegance. The main attraction is the magnificent **harbour**, built between 1817 and 1842 and enclosed by two granite piers stretching more than half a mile out to sea, each capped by a lighthouse. The piers are popular for fishing and bird-watching, or for merely idling about. The harbour, a major yachting centre, features the headquarters of several yacht clubs.

Dún Laoghaire's main thoroughfare, George's Street, runs parallel to the coast. Between here and the harbour, on Haigh Terrace, the old Mariners' Church, built in 1837, is now the home of the **National Maritime Museum** (open May–Sept Tues–Sun 1–5pm; admission fee). Among its models and memorabilia are a French longboat captured during Wolfe Tone's unsuccessful invasion of Bantry Bay in 1796, and the Baily

Left: the Martello Tower at Sandycove
Right: the harbour at Dún Laoghaire

excursions

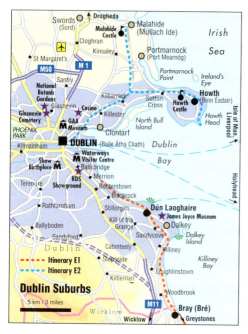

Optic, a huge clockwork-driven lighthouse lens from the Baily Lighthouse at Howth.

You can easily walk along the seafront to the next promontory at **Sandycove**, about ½ mile (1 km) away. Alternatively, you can take the DART. The rocky cove, known as the **Forty Foot Pool**, after the 40th Regiment of Foot that was formerly stationed in the area, was a traditional nude bathing spot for men. Today, both sexes brave the chilly waters – though nudity is banned after 9am.

The Martello Towers

Nearby is Sandycove's main attraction, the Martello tower that houses the **James Joyce Museum** (open Apr–Oct Mon–Sat 10am–1pm and 2–5pm, Sun and holidays 2–6pm; admission fee). The tower was one of 34 such defensive edifices built along Ireland's east and south coasts in 1804–15 to fend off a possible invasion by Napoleon. Joyce stayed here for a few days in 1904, long enough to find inspiration for the opening chapter of *Ulysses*; descriptions of the gun platform and living room are recognisable from the book. Letters, photographs, rare editions of Joyce's work, his death mask and personal possessions are among the items on display. When the weather is good there are fine views along the coast from the gun platform on the roof. Sandycove village, with its cafés, pubs and interesting boutiques, is a 15-minute walk inland.

Two more stops on the DART bring you to **Dalkey** (pronounced *Dawky*) whose narrow winding roads and Victorian villas make it the most attractive village along the south bay.

In the Middle Ages it had the only natural harbour on the east coast, and was the most prosperous port in Ireland. In those days it had no fewer than seven castles, of which Archibald's Castle and Goat's Castle still survive. Both date from the 15th or 16th century and are situated on the main road, Castle Street. Goat's Castle, now called **Dalkey Castle and Heritage Centre** (open

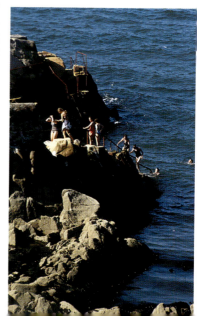

1. south along dublin bay

Apr–Oct Mon–Fri 9.30am–5pm, Sat–Sun 11am–5pm; Nov–Mar Sat–Sun 11am–5pm; admission fee), features displays on the history of the area and temporary arts and crafts exhibitions.

Dalkey has lots of good pubs and fine restaurants. Coliemore Road leads down to the harbour where, in summer, you can take a boat to **Dalkey Island**, a short distance offshore. The island has a bird sanctuary, another Martello tower and a medieval church.

From the harbour, Vico Road runs south along the cliffs overlooking **Killiney Bay**, with spectacular views of the coastline. If you're driving, head up to the top of Killiney Hill Park, where you can park and admire the sweeping view of the bay and the Wicklow Mountains. Many of Killiney's exclusive homes are owned by international celebrities – film directors, actors, rock stars and writers – but anyone can enjoy the wide beach that runs the length of the bay.

A Victorian Seaside Resort

James Joyce lived in **Bray** from 1888 to 1891, when it was an elegant, Victorian seaside resort. But most of its old character was lost in the rapid expansion that created Dublin's commuter belt. Today it has a rather tacky air, its promenade lined with amusement arcades and fast-food outlets, though the beach still draws large crowds, especially families, in summer. The **National Sea-Life Centre** (open daily 10am–5pm; admission fee), an aquarium focusing on Irish marine species, is particularly popular with children.

For walking enthusiasts, the 'Slí na Sláinte – The Healthy Walk' is an 8¾-mile (14-km) coastal and urban route in and around the town. For a slightly shorter walk that escapes the crowds, take the bracing cliff walk along **Bray Head**, which rises steeply 790ft (241 metres) above the sea. The headland runs for 5 miles (8 km) south to Greystones and affords more fabulous views of mountains and sea. You can then catch the DART back to Dublin from Greystones.

Left: making waves at Forty Foot Pool
Above: gnomic goings on at Bray

2. North Along Dublin Bay (see map, p54)

A day-long excursion around the bay north of Dublin, incorporating lovely walks from the seaside town of Howth and the 12th-century castle at Malahide.

The DART train runs north to the terminus on the Howth branch line. Change at Howth Junction for Malahide. Get an up-to-date timetable for these routes to avoid long waits at Howth Junction, where there are no facilities. Both towns can also be reached by bus.

The DART train is a quick and cheap way to get out of the city centre; in less than an hour you can be walking along the cliffs of Howth Head. Heading north, the DART passes through the historically significant town of **Clontarf**. King Brian Boru beat off the Viking army here in 1014 but there is not much to see nowadays. The DART continues north to Howth Junction where the line splits, so make sure you are on the branch for Howth.

At **Howth** (rhymes with 'both'), turn left out of the station. Howth Harbour is on your left and to the right is the uphill slope of Church Street, which leads to the heart of the town. The Gothic ruins of St Mary's Abbey, dating from 1235, overlook the harbour. You might want to take a walk along one of the piers, with a backdrop of boats bobbing in Howth Harbour. This was Dublin's main harbour for boats from England until trade shifted to Dún Laoghaire in 1833.

Return to the promenade and turn left to continue walking, with Balscadden Bay on your left. As Balscadden Road skirts the bay and wends its way uphill, look on your left for Balscadden House. A plaque on the wall honours W.B. Yeats, who lived in the house from 1880 to 1883.

Above: glowering skies at Howth Harbour
Left: whiling away a moment at a Malahide pub

2. north along dublin bay

Howth Cliff Walk

Continue on the path out of the car park at the far end, which takes you to the Nose of Howth then south along the headland. The **Howth Cliff Walk** is a delight on a good day and anyone in comfortable shoes can easily negotiate the well-defined track. The path leads for 2½ miles (4 km) above cliffs with views south to the Wicklow Mountains; below, gulls and cormorants fly over the waves. The path heads towards the Baily Lighthouse, the last manned lighthouse in Ireland until it was automated in 1997.

There are some steep paths that branch off to the right, leading up to the summit. By keeping straight ahead you emerge at a road. To the left is the lighthouse, and though this section of the path is marked 'Private Property' many locals walk to the end. Turning right and keeping right would lead back to Howth via the road, but it is much more satisfying to retrace your steps along the magnificent cliffs. Catch the DART back to Howth Junction and change platforms for the Malahide train.

Malahide and its Castle

Malahide is a pretty little seaside town, with guesthouses, restaurants, stylish shops and a small marina, reached by walking out of the DART station and turning left at the main road; turning right takes you to the town's main attraction, Malahide Castle. The main entrance to the castle and its 250-acre (100-ha) grounds, is on the left. Paths lead through woods until you reach the castle buildings. The paths are signposted and on a sunny day you can make the most of your visit by meandering through the grounds. Before reaching the castle you will find the entrance to the **Fry Model Railway** (open Apr–Oct Mon–Sat 10am–1pm and 2–5pm, Sun and holidays 2–6pm; Nov–Mar Sat–Sun and holidays 2– 5pm; admission fee). Tours (at a quarter-to and quarter-past the hour) of Ireland's largest model railway, complete with narration, lead you around the impressive layout. They tell the history of the country's railways and trams, with models of various parts of the country, especially Dublin, through which immaculate 'O' gauge trains run.

From 1185 until 1975 **Malahide Castle** (open Apr–Oct Mon–Sat 10am–5pm, Sun and holidays 11.30am–6pm; Nov–Mar Mon–Fri 10am–5pm, Sat–Sun and holidays 2–5pm; admission fee) was the home of the Talbot family, who came from Normandy in France. Tours of the castle leave from the main entrance at regular intervals, and take about 30–40 minutes. In each room a recorded commentary describes the main features. The Oak Room has beautiful, dark carved wood panels and a splendid 1812 fireplace. The west wing has walls up to 8ft (2.5 metres) thick, and in the small drawing room there is a magnificent 1760 mirror hanging over the Italian marble fireplace.

Right: Malahide Castle

58 excursions

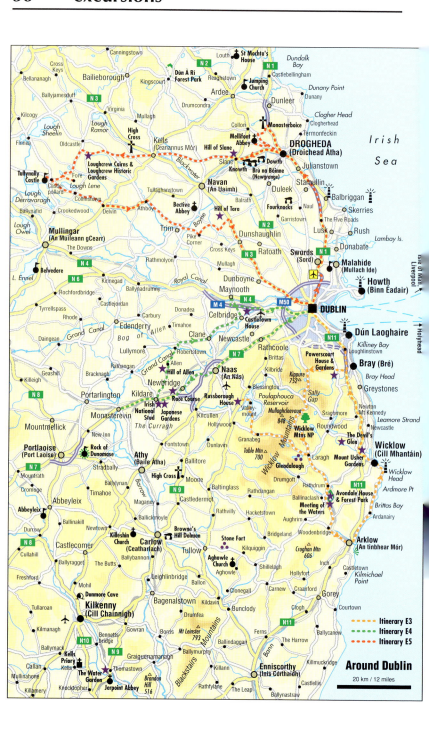

3. wicklow mountains

The tour takes in the great drawing room, the children's and master bedrooms and most impressive of all, the great hall, dating from about 1475. The hall, which has a minstrels' gallery, still hosts banquets. Oliver Cromwell stayed here in the mid-17th century during the Siege of Dublin, when his Ironside army slaughtered its way through the country, and a portrait of the Lord Protector, as his official title had it, hangs on the walls. A curiosity in one corner is Puck's Door, named for the ghost of a servant who hanged himself after falling asleep and allowing invaders into the house.

From May to September the Talbot Botanical Gardens in the castle grounds are open to the public. Laid out in the mid-20th century by Lord Milo Talbot, the gardens have more than 5,000 species of plants from around the world.

Allow about 15 minutes to return to Malahide station to catch the DART train back to central Dublin.

3. Around the Wicklow Mountains
(see map, p58)

The stunning landscape of the Wicklow Mountains lies at Dublin's back door, with stately homes, gardens and an ancient monastic site dotted around a scenic drive. On a day-trip, you'll have time to see two of the major sights; an overnight excursion allows for more leisurely walks.

The major sites can be reached on coach tours from Dublin. The most direct route if you are driving from Dublin is the N11 (M11) south.

County Wicklow is known as the Garden of Ireland. Stretching from the western foothills of the Wicklow Mountains to the sandy beaches of the Irish Sea, it encompasses an ever-changing landscape of lush forests, heather-covered, windswept moors, peaceful lakes and thundering waterfalls.

About 15 miles (24 km) south of Dublin, just beyond Bray, take the exit for Enniskerry and follow signs to **Powerscourt House and Gardens** (open daily 9.30am–5.30pm; winter times may vary; admission fee). The Powerscourt estate, one of the finest in the country, takes its name from the le Poer family, whose castle stood here in 1300. The lands were granted to an Englishman, Richard Wingfield, in 1603, and in the 18th century the castle was transformed into an elegant mansion by the architect, Richard Castle. The building was gutted by a fire in 1974 and, although the splendid ceiling of the ballroom has now been restored, there is little to see inside, other than a film and exhibition on its former glory.

The real attraction is the magnificent gardens. From the rear of the stately shell there is a grand view of the Wicklow landmark, Great Sugar Loaf Mountain. A flight of

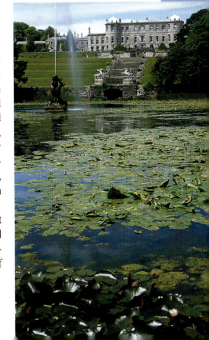

Right: the Triton Lake at Powerscourt Gardens, with the grand house as a backdrop

steps leads down the terraces to the Triton Lake, with a fountain and heraldic winged horses. It's worth taking the time to stroll through the 47-acre (19-ha) demesne, whose features include Japanese, Italian and walled gardens. There is also a good café and restaurant. About 3 miles (5 km) away is the **Powerscourt Waterfall**, the country's highest. There are hiking trails and picnic areas around the falls.

Return to the delightful village of **Enniskerry** and follow signs for Glencree Drive. After about 5½ miles (9 km), turn left on to the R115 towards Sally Gap. This is the old Military Road, built by the British to aid their pursuit of Irish rebels hiding in the mountains after an uprising in 1798. At a fork in the road, veer right; as the road rises above the valley the landscape changes to bleak moorland. The only sign of civilisation is at the **Sally Gap** crossroads, 5 miles (8 km) on. Continue straight ahead; the route becomes greener just before the **Glenmacnass Waterfall**. The road descends into the tiny village of **Laragh**.

Turn right to reach nearby **Glendalough**, one of Ireland's finest early Christian monastic sites. The Visitor Centre (open Jun–Aug daily 9am–6.30pm; Sept–mid-Oct and mid-Mar–May 9.30am–6pm; mid-Oct–mid-Mar 9.30am–5pm; admission fee) has a museum documenting the founding of the monastery by St Kevin in the 6th century. There is no charge to wander around the grounds, where you can see the fine 100- ft (30-metre) round tower, the remains of the cathedral and smaller churches.

Wicklow National Park

Glendalough is part of the vast **Wicklow National Park**. A path leads over a bridge and along the 'valley of two lakes', from which the site takes its name. There are more monastic ruins around the Upper Lake, and a small visitor centre. The hiking trails that lead up into the mountains afford some fantastic views. Continue west on the R756 towards Hollywood, which runs through beautiful parkland and windy **Wicklow Gap**. Beyond, take the right-hand fork, signposted Valleymount, which takes you on a beautiful lakeside drive along the Poulaphouca Reservoir to Blessington.

Three miles (5 km) south of town, on the main road, is **Russborough House** (open May–Sept daily 10.30am–5.30pm; Apr and Oct Sun and holidays; admission fee). Built in the 1740s, this Palladian mansion was designed by Richard Castle and is one of the grandest in the country. Highlights of the interior include elaborate stucco ceilings,

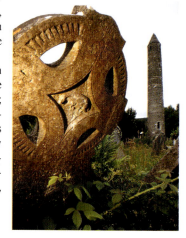

Above: Powerscourt Waterfall.
Right: the round tower at Glendalough

4. county kildare

inlaid floors, silver and tapestries. Sir Alfred Beit bought the house in 1952 as a home for his art collection, but after three robberies, Beit donated many of the paintings to the National Gallery. A selection of Spanish, Dutch and other masterpieces remain on display.

The return to Dublin is only 19 miles (30 km) on the N81. Or take the R410 from Blessington to Naas for the tour of County Kildare *(see below)*. For an alternative scenic route, head south from Laragh on the R755 through pretty Clara Vale to Rathdrum, and continue on the R752 through the delightful Vale of Avoca. At Woodenbridge, turn left on the R747 to Arklow, then head north on R750 along the coast, past the white-sand beach at Brittas Bay. Outside Wicklow Town get on the N11 back to Dublin.

4. COUNTY KILDARE *(see map, p58)*

A drive through the broad, green pastures of Kildare, heart of Ireland's horse-racing and breeding country.

You can visit the National Stud and Japanese Gardens on a coach tour from Dublin. The town of Kildare is 30 miles (48 km) from Dublin on the N7 (M7).

Ireland has produced some of the world's top racehorses, and the centre of this thoroughbred world is the grassy, limestone plain of the Curragh. The origins of the sport date back to prehistoric times, when business was conducted, marriages celebrated, laws codified and alliances formed at great fairs. Games were staged at these events; horse-racing was the most popular event.

One of the region's racecourses is in **Naas**, the county's largest town, and major business and sporting centre, which is quickly reached from Dublin. Another is at Punchestown, 3 miles (5 km) southeast. A few miles southwest, beyond Newbridge, is the **Curragh**. This sweeping, unfenced field covers more than 5,000 acres (2,000 ha). Some say this pasture is so good for grazing horses because the grass from the limestone plain is the best for building bone. The country's biggest racing event, the Irish Derby, takes place at the Curragh racecourse.

Nearby **Kildare**'s main sight, **St Brigid's Cathedral** (open Mon–Sat 10am–1pm and 2–5pm, Sun 2–5pm; donation), stands adjacent to the tiny, triangular town square. St Brigid, one of Ireland's patron saints, founded a religious community for both men and women here in 490. It was called *Cill Dara* (Church of the Oak), from which the town takes its name. The present church dates from the 13th century. The churchyard contains the remains of a pit in which a sacred perpetual fire burned; it remained alight until the 16th century. The splendid, round 12th-century tower is, at 108 ft (33 metres), the second-highest in the country. Climb to the top for great views.

Right: Kildare's racehorses have the choicest grazing grounds in the country

South of town, the **Irish National Stud** (open Feb–Nov 9.30am–6pm; admission fee), a state-run, thoroughbred breeding farm, was established in 1900 by Colonel William Hall-Walker, son of a Scottish brewer. Views on his breeding methods ranged from inspired to eccentric – he read each foal's horoscope to decide which ones to train for big races. In 1915 he presented the stud farm to the British crown, which handed it over to the Irish nation in 1943. An entertaining 40-minute tour explains the workings of the National Stud, and the process of breeding a winner. You can walk through the grounds and watch the horses exercising in their paddocks. There is also a museum, and the **Japanese Gardens** created by Hall-Walker's Japanese gardener, Tassa Eida. Laid out along paths to represent stages in the life of man, the gardens contain rare plants, bridges and cavernous passages.

The National Stud's newest addition, **St Fiachra's Garden**, is named after a 6th-century Irish monk who became the patron saint of gardeners. Wide paths lead through woodland and along a lake to a reconstruction of a monastic cell, which contains a Waterford crystal garden.

Monasterevin

Six miles (10 km) from Kildare, **Monasterevin** is a sleepy market town that was once home to the tenor John McCormack. It was a prosperous place in the 18th century due to its position at the place where the Grand Canal enters the River Barrow. Turn right at the traffic lights to see the aqueduct, built in 1829–31 to ease the passage of water traffic through the town. **Robertstown**, north of Kildare, is another pretty canal town with 19th-century warehouses and cottages along the waterside. Barge cruises operate from the quay.

A detour to Celbridge, on the R403/R405, takes you to **Castletown House** (open Jun–Sept Mon–Fri 10am–6pm, Sat–Sun 1–6pm; Oct Mon–Fri 10am–5pm, Sun 1–5pm; Nov Sun 1–5pm; Apr–May Sun 1–6pm; admission fee), possibly the finest Palladian mansion in Ireland. It was built for William Connolly,

Speaker of the Irish House of Commons, in 1722–32 and designed by Italian architect Alessandro Galilei. You can see the magnificent interior on a guided tour. Highlights include the rococo stucco-work, the Long Gallery with its Pompeii-style murals, and the Print Room, with prints pasted directly onto the wall, the country's only surviving example of this 18th-century fashion. Return to Dublin via the M4/N4.

Above: Kildare's Japanese Gardens
Left: a canal boat at Robertstown

5. the boyne drive

5. The Boyne Drive *(see map, p58)*

A drive through the historic Boyne Valley, with its prehistoric sites and monastic monuments, to the idyllic rolling hills and tranquil lakes of Westmeath. Allow two days to explore the area's Celtic treasures.

Organised coach trips run from Dublin to Brú na Bóinne and other attractions. A rental car, however, will allow you to spend more time at the sites. Some of them lie along winding country roads and can be a little tricky to find, so ask for directions locally.

The River Boyne, which was sacred to the Celts, meanders its way through several counties north of Dublin. This valley was the cradle of Irish civilisation, where Neolithic farmers built sophisticated tombs, and kings were crowned. The Battle of the Boyne in 1690, a turning point in Irish history, solidified English rule.

The town of **Drogheda**, about an hour's drive north of Dublin on the N1, is set along the banks of the river and has an attractive medieval centre. St Lawrence Gate, a handsome, 13th-century barbican, is the only remnant of its ancient walls. More than 3,000 Drogheda citizens were killed during Cromwell's vicious campaign against the Irish in 1649. Catholic persecution continued with the martyrdom of Oliver Plunkett in 1681; his mummified head is displayed in St Peter's Church. Country roads north of Drogheda lead to **Monasterboice**. Amid the ruins of a 5th-century monastery are three sculpted High Crosses. Muiredach's Cross, with its outstanding carved biblical scenes, and the West Cross, the tallest in Ireland, are among the finest of their kind. There is also a round tower and two ruined churches.

A few miles southwest are the remains of **Mellifont Abbey** (open May–Oct daily 10am–6pm; admission fee), Ireland's first Cistercian monastery, founded in 1142. After its dissolution in 1539 it became a fortified house, and William of Orange set up his headquarters here during the Battle of the Boyne. Its most impressive feature is the octagonal *lavabo*, where the monks washed before meals.

Signposted off the N51 west of Drogheda, **Oldbridge** marks the site of the Battle of the Boyne, where William of Orange defeated the deposed Catholic king, James II, and his poorly-trained force of Irish and French soldiers. You can follow a pretty riverside drive past the battle sites.

Newgrange

Further west off the N51 are the great passage tombs at **Brú na Bóinne,** also known as Newgrange (open Jun–mid-Sept 9am–7pm, late Sept and May 9am–6.30pm; Oct and Mar–Apr 9.30am–5.30pm; Nov–Feb 9.30am–5pm; admission fee). Its Celtic name, 'Dwelling Place of the Boyne', describes an area bounded on three sides by the river. Within it are some 50 prehistoric burial

Right: Muiredach's Cross, with carved biblical scenes, at Monasterboice

chambers, built by Neolithic farmers over 5,000 years ago, most of which lie on private land and are not accessible. But the three largest tombs – Newgrange, Knowth and Dowth (closed) – are among the most important archaeological sites in the world. Dowth is closed and Newgrange and Knowth can be visited on guided tours only. These leave from the Visitor Centre, which screens an excellent film and has informative background exhibits. Arrive early as this is a busy site and tour numbers are limited; the last tour commences 90 minutes before closing time.

The enormous, 36-ft (11-meter) mound of Newgrange covers more than an acre (0.5 ha) and was built from over 200,000 tons of earth and stone. A decorated entrance stone marks the long, narrow passage leading into a burial chamber topped by a high, corbelled roof. The chamber's most amazing feature is the 'roof box', a small opening above the door that allows a beam of sunlight to reach the back of the chamber at dawn on the winter solstice – possibly a powerful symbol of rebirth. The effect is recreated for visitors.

Knowth is a larger site, with 18 'satellite' tombs encircling the main central grave. Its construction is unusual, with two separate passages leading into unconnected burial chambers. Knowth has a superb display of megalithic art – there are some 300 decorated stones in the main mound alone, many of which can be seen outside the tomb. A place of settlement as well as burial, Knowth served as home to the high kings in the early Christian period, and was occupied well into Norman times.

St Patrick and the Fire

Continue west on the N51 to Slane, and turn right on the N2 to the **Hill of Slane**. Here, in 433, St Patrick lit the paschal fire to celebrate the arrival of Christianity in Ireland. A fire is still lit here every Easter. The remains of 16th-century Slane Abbey stand on the hilltop, where there are great views across the Boyne Valley.

To avoid possible traffic hold-ups at Navan, take the smaller R163 to **Kells**, famous for the monastery founded by St Colmcille (Columba). Monks fled to the monastery from Iona after Viking attacks in the 9th century, and it is thought they completed the magnificent Book of Kells *(see page 22)* here. St Columba's Church stands on the original site of the monastery. In its grounds are a 10th-century round tower, and four High Crosses. The

Above: Mellifont Abbey in the Boyne Valley
Right: carvings on one of the Loughcrew Cairns

5. the boyne drive

Market Cross, which was moved to the town centre in 1798 and used as a gallows, is now outside the Kells Heritage Centre. Near the church is an old stone oratory known as St Colmcille's House.

Take the R163 and R154 west towards Oldcastle. Outside town are the **Loughcrew Cairns** (open mid-Jun–mid-Sept 10am–6pm), which are less visited and more peaceful than Brú na Bóinne. This group of 30 Stone Age cairns is the largest in Ireland, spread across three peaks of the Loughcrew Hills. The main Cairn T, a large passage tomb, is reached up a steep hill. Access to the site is not restricted, and outside summer months you can get a key to enter the cairn nearby at **Loughcrew Gardens** (open Apr–Sept daily noon–6pm; Oct–Mar Sat, Sun noon–4pm; admission fee). Among the features of these lovely gardens, which date from the 17th century, are a Yew Walk and a fairy garden.

The Hamlet of Fore

Head south on the R195 towards Castlepollard for a highly recommended visit to the tiny hamlet of **Fore**, just off the road. Nestled between the hills, Fore has 'Seven Wonders' – such as water that flows uphill – associated with St Feichin, who founded a monastery here in the 7th century. The ruins of an early 13th-century Benedictine Abbey stand majestically in a field. This lovely, rural corner of County Westmeath also has several lakes and is a good place to break your journey. Outside **Castlepollard**, Tullynally Castle is one of the largest castles in the country that still serves as a family home. The castle is open in summer only (check times locally) but its woodlands and gardens are open all year.

Take the R395 to Athboy and turn right on the R154 to the town of **Trim**. Its impressive Anglo-Norman castle (open mid-Jun–mid-Sept daily 10am–6pm; admission fee), set along the Boyne, is the largest in Ireland. It was built by Hugh de Lacy in 1173 and most of its original features remain. The Hollywood blockbuster *Braveheart*, starring Mel Gibson, was shot here. It's well worth taking the tour of the keep to see the four interconnecting towers, and there is a fantastic view from the top. On the opposite bank of the river is the Yellow Steeple, the belfry tower of a ruined abbey that was destroyed during Cromwell's campaign.

The Trim Tourist Office can give you precise directions to the **Hill of Tara** (open mid-Jun–Oct daily 10am–6pm; admission fee). This, the most sacred site of ancient Ireland, was the main cultural and religious centre until the arrival of Christianity, and served as the high kings' coronation site. To understand the importance of the hollows and mounds, which are all that remain of Tara's former glory, take a tour from the Visitor Centre. It is a short drive back to Dublin on the N3.

Right: Hill of Tara, the most sacred site in ancient Ireland

ONDON BELFAS

Leisure Activities

SHOPPING

From the latest fashions to the finest Irish crafts, you'll find good shopping throughout Dublin city centre. Most shops are open Monday to Saturday, from 9 or 9.30am until 5.30 or 6pm. On Thursday some stores are open until 8 or 9pm. Many also open on Sunday afternoon, and there are late-night grocery and 24-hour shops. Most large stores accept major credit cards such as Visa and MasterCard; some also accept traveller's cheques, if you have your passport for identification.

Sales tax (VAT) is included in the price. Visitors from outside the EU may be able to reclaim this tax, though it may not be worth the hassle on smaller purchases. If you ship goods home from the store, you can reclaim the tax at point of purchase. Otherwise, look for the Cashback logo in shops, fill out the form and take it to the Cashback offices at Dublin airport before departure.

Where to Shop

There are two major shopping districts in Dublin. The pedestrian-only **Grafton Street** and its side streets constitute the more upmarket end for clothing and gifts. Despite the influx of UK chain stores, numerous buskers, flower stalls and pavement toy sellers help the neighbourhood retain its old character. Here, too, is **Brown Thomas**, the city's famous department store, which sells posh clothes, accessories and designer wear.

Another of the few remaining Irish department stores, **Clery's**, is on O'Connell Street. But **Henry Street** (pedestrianised) and **Mary Street** form the main shopping area north of the Liffey. The stores lining this long thoroughfare are less trendy and may offer better value. **Arnott's**, another local department store, is located here.

Tucked around **Temple Bar** are trendy gift shops and boutiques, as well as art and design outlets. **South Great George's Street** has some one-of-a-kind shops, such as the **Dolls' Hospital**, which sells porcelain dolls and teddy bears.

Shopping Centres

Dublin has several indoor shopping malls. The largest is **St Stephen's Green Shopping Centre** at the bottom end of Grafton Street. The **Powerscourt Centre**, in a refurbished townhouse, has antiques, boutiques and an art gallery. The nearby **Westbury Centre**, in Harry Street, sells clothes, carpets and lingerie. Off Grafton Street, **Royal Hibernian Way** is a small arcade whose exclusive shops sell Leonidas chocolates and menswear. Shops in the **Ilac Centre**, Henry Street, and the **Jervis Centre**, Mary Street, sell a range of clothing and home wares.

Markets

Dublin's main fruit, vegetable and flower market is on **Moore Street** (open daily 10am–6pm). A food market selling organic and home-produced goods is held on Saturday in **Temple Bar**'s Meeting House Square. In **George Street Market Arcade** (open daily) you'll find everything from fashions to fortune-tellers, candles to collectibles and second-hand records and books. Similar goods can be found at **Mother Redcap's Market** in Back Lane (open Fri–Sun 11am–5.30pm).

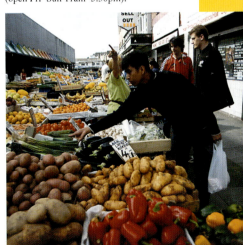

Left: leisure time in Wicklow
Right: Moore Street Market in Dublin

leisure activities

Irish Goods and Crafts

Irish crafts are generally well made and show a high degree of workmanship. Many incorporate traditional Celtic motifs into contemporary designs. The country has also long been known for its textile industry. Traditional tweeds and woollens are good buys, and old, homespun styles have been updated to reflect the latest fashions.

Delicate Irish linen and lace are also renowned. Some of the most beautiful scarves, shawls and woven goods come from the Avoca Handweavers mill in County Wicklow. There is an **Avoca** shop on Suffolk Street. **Nassau Street** has several shops specialising in Irish tweeds and knitwear, including **Kevin & Howlin**, **Blarney Woollen Mills**, **House of Ireland** and **The Kilkenny Shop**.

These shops also sell a range of other fine Irish crafts, including hand-blown glassware and cut crystal. Waterford Crystal is one of the most famous brands. Pottery and ceramics are also beautifully produced in both traditional and contemporary designs.

DESIGNyard in Temple Bar sells a wide selection of contemporary Irish jewellery. On the first floor is the **Craft Council of Ireland**'s retail gallery, where traditional techniques are used to produce contemporary fashions and home furnishings.

The **Whichcraft Gallery** on Lord Edward Street, near Dublin Castle, is another good outlet for modern Irish crafts. The **Original Print Gallery** in Temple Bar sells contemporary prints and etchings. **The Bridge** gallery on Upper Ormond Quay sells a range of Irish artwork. Many artists also display their works on the railings around **Merrion Square** at the weekends, and though the quality varies, some of it is surprisingly good.

Other items

Irish music provides a wonderful array of original souvenirs. You can buy instruments from a penny whistle to a *bodhrán* (hand-held drum) at **Walton's** on South Great George's Street. For CDs, try **Celtic Note** on Nassau Street.

Museum gift shops are a good place to find quality gifts and souvenirs with an Irish theme, such as illustrated books and stationery. **Antiques** can be found on Francis Street, in the Powerscourt Centre, and at shops along the quays.

Top: antiques in Baggotrath Place
Left: modernity at DESIGNyard, Temple Bar

… ting out in Dublin has never been better. … ot long ago, the number of international-… ass restaurants was limited, but then came … e Celtic Tiger effect. The influx of money, … urists and international companies has … eated a food boom. It is therefore worth … oking ahead for a table at the upscale … teries, especially at the weekends.

Dublin weekends start on a Thursday, … te-night shopping day, when many restau-… nts are full in the early evening. Friday … d Saturday are busy, and although some … aces do close on Sunday, you will have … o trouble finding somewhere to eat.

Lunch is usually from about noon to … 30pm. By 6pm some places will start to fill … ith diners encouraged by 'early bird' … enus. Meals are served until about 10pm, … though there are plenty of places that stay … pen much later.

Every cuisine in the world is now in … ublin, and there are plenty of fast-food out-… ts. Many pubs serve food *(see Nightlife, … age 74)*, and standards are higher than ever. … pub lunch is a good way to break the day, … ut at weekends especially, pubs can be … acked so you will need to find a table early.

The national cuisine includes great-… uality salmon, scallops and oysters, prime … eef, lamb and farmhouse cheeses, along-… ide traditional dishes. One such dish is … ublin Coddle. This is a hearty Saturday … ight stew of bacon, sausages and/or ham … ith potatoes and onions. Or try Boxty, a … ancake filled with almost anything, but … sually meat or fish with potatoes, onions … nd vegetables.

Inevitably, the country's favourite … egetable, the potato, is a major ingredient … n many recipes, such as Colcannon, a … ashed cabbage, potato and leek dish; and … Champ, which uses potatoes and scallions … (spring onions).

The streets of Temple Bar are packed with pubs and restaurants. The Grafton Street area, particularly near St Stephen's Green and around Chatham Street, is also good for eating out. Another recommended option is an area roughly bounded by Dame Street, South Great George's Street and William Street South.

Right: pub grub writ large

Prices
Eating out is not cheap; prices are comparable to those of any northern European capital city. The price brackets below indicate the approximate cost of a three-course dinner for two, with house wine.
$ = under 40 Euros (IR£50)
$$ – from 40–60 Euros (IR£50–75)
$$$ – over 60 Euros (IR£75)

In the City
Upscale Eateries
The Commons
86 St Stephen's Green
Tel: 01-475 2597
The former dining room of University College, The Commons exudes a convivial, old-world atmosphere. The wide-ranging cuisine, which has been awarded a Michelin star, changes daily, and might include grilled shark served with peppered carrot, or unusual specialities such as loin of rabbit with Dublin Bay prawns. $$$

Cooke's Café
14 South William Street
Tel: 01-679 0536
A casual appearance and atmosphere belie the standards of the open-plan kitchen in this bistro-style eatery. There is seating outside, and a more formal Rhino Room restaurant above. Specialises in a mix of Cal-Ital and other styles, ranging from simple pastas to grilled duck with *pancetta* and Marsala balsamic sauce. Moderate lunch and early-bird menus. $$$

Les Frères Jacques
74 Dame Street
Tel: 01-679 4555
Long-established, sophisticated French restaurant, opposite Dublin Castle. Seafood is a speciality – the lobsters in the tank are destined to be flambéed in whiskey. Roast Wicklow lamb cooked in its own juices is but one of the tasty options served up by the French staff. $$$

Peacock Alley
Fitzwilliam Hotel, 128 St Stephen's Green
Tel: 01-677 0708
Char-grilled guinea fowl with saffron risotto is typical of the Mediterranean-influenced dishes on offer here, and that is just a starter. The minimalist white walls are softened by flowers on the tables and a view over St Stephen's Green from the top of the Fitzwilliam Hotel. Chef Conrad Gallagher continues to exert his influence on Dublin's restaurant scene. $$$

Restaurant Patrick Guilbaud
21 Merrion Street Upper
Tel: 01-677 3363
One of the country's best restaurants, Michelin-starred and based in an 18th-century Georgian townhouse alongside the Merrion Hotel. The affordable fixed-price lunch menu is a good way to sample the superb contemporary French cuisine, such as *troncon* of wild sea bass *meunière*. $$$

Thornton's
1 Portobello Road
Tel: 01-454 9067
Kevin Thornton, one of Dublin's fine contemporary chefs, fuses Irish ingredients with French flair in a formal but cool dining room, that is candle-lit at night. Adventurous gourmets should go for the 'Surprise' menu, which will bring six stunning courses to your table. $$$

Local Flavours
L'Ecrivain
One of the best places in the city for new Irish cuisine combined with a flavour of France. L'Ecrivain combines formality and relaxation in a bright modern space. Homemade breads set the tone for dishes such as

the signature starter of oysters with bacon, cabbage and a Guinness *sabayon*, or breast of guinea fowl with a black pudding mousse. The restaurant is also famous for its fish dishes, with catches from all over Ireland arriving the day it is netted. $$$

Gallagher's Boxty House
20–21 Temple Bar
Tel: 01-677 2762
Boxty (stuffed pancakes) is a firm favourite here, and other Irish dishes are also available. It's always busy, and you might find yourself sharing one of the long wooden tables. Brisk service, and hearty fare if not *haute cuisine*. No advance bookings are taken, but you can reserve a table on the evening itself. $

Lord Edward
23 Christchurch Place
Tel: 01-454 2420
Dublin's oldest seafood restaurant has intimate little rooms on three floors. Offers fresh lobster, salmon and other local fish, including a dozen sole recipes and Dublin Bay prawns cooked in seven different ways. $$$

Roly's Bistro
7 Ballsbridge Terrace
Tel: 01-668 2611
Busy bistro near the American Embassy in Ballsbridge, featuring Irish flavours and

Above: a beautifully presented dish

restaurants

any other cuisines too: Clonakilty black pudding wrapped in brioche gives an idea of the fusion of flavours. Usually noisy and boisterous, with an affordable wide-ranging wine list, excellent service and imaginative cooking. $$

European and Fusion

Belgo
17–19 Sycamore Street
Tel: 01-672 7555
Set in a spacious and high-ceilinged room in Temple Bar, this branch of the Belgo chain is a great place for a coffee, a light meal (try the £5 lunchtime bargain), something from the seafood menu or one of the numerous Belgian beers, sold on draught or by the bottle. $$

Bruno's
30 East Essex Street
Tel: 01-670 6767
This small but light, bright and affordable establishment is always busy. Its French-Mediterranean menu offers a good range of tasty combinations such as a delicious spinach and goat-cheese tart or oak-smoked beef served with crushed Parma ham potatoes. $$

Eden
Meeting House Square
Tel: 01-670 5373
Bright and airy restaurant with lots of greenery and a great location, with some tables on Meeting House Square itself. A menu as contemporary as the decor includes such dishes as pan-fried crab claws or organic pork and apricot stew with mash, herbs and red-wine gravy. $$$

Fitzers
51 Dawson Street
Tel: 01-677 1155
Stylish yet casual fusion restaurant mixing Italian, Californian and Asian influences, with Thai noodles, salmon and pasta all on the bistro-style menu. The interior is light and bright, and there's a heated seating area outside, where you can just have a coffee except during busy meal times. Branches in Temple House Square and in the National Gallery. $$

Gotham Café
8 South Anne Street
Tel: 01-679 5266
Busy place that is either a café or restaurant depending on the time of day. Often fully booked in the evening due to a great range of pizzas and mouthwatering dishes such as honey-roasted pork with basil-mash and oven-roasted vegetables. $$

Little Caesar's Palace
5 Balfe Street
Tel: 01-671 8714
Compact and always packed, this place is well worth queuing for. The pizzas are excellent: watch the chef spin the dough and prepare and cook the pizza. $$

Mermaid Café
69–70 Dame Street
Tel: 01-670 8236
This Temple Bar restaurant features superb service and mainly Mediterranean-style cooking, though New England crab cakes have become a signature dish. The seafood, especially the Giant Atlantic Seafood Casserole, is generally excellent, and the portions are generous. The café is small, so booking is usually essential. $$

Pasta Fresca
2–4 Chatham Street
Tel: 01-679 2402
One of several good pizza places in close proximity to one another, Pasta Fresca serves home-made pastas and a range of scrummy, good-value pizzas virtually all day. The atmosphere is lively, the service brisk, and there's usually a fast-moving queue for the tables. $

Right: a good place for a pizza

eating out

Pizza Stop
6–10 Chatham Lane
Tel: 01-679 6712
This ever-busy, ever-noisy Italian restaurant serves above-average pizzas and delicious pasta dishes: one to try is the chicken *parmegiano*. $

World Cuisine
Acapulco
7 South Great George's Street
Tel: 01-677 1085
Offers excellent Tex-Mex cooking – with tasty *enchilladas*, wonderful chicken *fajitas*, *nachos*, *burritos* and the like – served in a bustling dining room, or you could choose the galleried seating area. There are some lovely, colourful Mexican paintings on the walls. Refreshing margaritas come by the pitcher. $

Café Mao
2–3 Chatham Row
Tel: 01-670 4899
Fashionable and lively Asian fusion restaurant featuring portraits of Chairman Mao. Tasty dishes include steamed rice paper trout. Portions are large, and the place tends to get noisy. It doesn't accept reservations so expect to queue at busy periods; turnover is fairly brisk. $

Cedar Tree
11 St Andrew's Street
Tel: 01-677 2121
Popular Lebanese restaurant that's open till late, when the cosy basement dining room is usually packed and lively. Try a range of *meze* dishes if you want to sample lots of different things, or opt for a tasty chicken dish. Lots of vegetarian options. $$

Wagamama
South King Street
Tel: 01-478 2152
Noisy offshoot of the popular London noodle restaurant, Wagamama is like a canteen where conversation echoes off every surface. Speedy, friendly service and a good choice of noodles, *teriyaki* and main courses such as chicken *katsu* curry and seafood with noodles. $$

Yamamori Noodles
71–72 South Great George's Street
Tel: 01-475 5001
The Yamamori is one of *the* places to hang out, especially if you want a cheap and filling lunch. Dinner is a little pricier, but the place is fun and constantly busy. Wide range of *sushi*, *sashimi*, noodles and other dishes in huge helpings. $

Café-Restaurants
Bad Ass Café
9–11 Crown Alley
Tel: 01-671 2596
A popular Temple Bar original that opened in 1986, long before the neighbourhood's redevelopment. The large, cavernous room is always buzzing; Bad Ass burgers and pizzas typify the fast-food style menu, though there's much else besides, including pasta and salads. Sinead O'Connor used to be a waitress here. $

Bewley's Oriental Café
78 Grafton Street
Tel: 01-635 5470
Almost as popular an attraction as the Book of Kells, Bewley's has been here since 1840 and there are several outlets around the city. A warren of rooms on several floors feature

restaurants

stained-glass windows and dark-wood panelling. You can have anything from a coffee to a full meal, although the menu is simple. Great place to take a break and read the paper. $

Busyfeet and Coco
42–42 South William Street
Tel: 01-671 9514
Open for breakfast, lunch and in the early evening, with home-made soups, salads, pastries and a large choice of coffees, teas and fruit cocktails. A relaxing place where locals drink their *latte* and read the newspapers. $

Café en Seine
40 Dawson Street
Tel: 01-677 4369
This large café has been popular since it opened 10 years ago and is especially busy on Sunday afternoon when it has live jazz and a late brunch menu. Lots of great salads, quiches, pasta, steaks and other simple dishes. $

Kilkenny Restaurant and Café
6 Nassau Street
Tel: 01-677 7066
Located on the first floor of the Kilkenny arts and crafts shop, overlooking Trinity College, this is a popular meeting place. It is bright and modern, with several café and restaurant areas adjacent to each other. Have a cappuccino or a glass of wine, a *pannini*, or maybe a salmon and spinach quiche. There are plenty of vegetarian options, and everything has a home-baked look. $

Outside Dublin

Brasserie Na Mara
1 Harbour Road, Dún Laoghaire
Tel: 01-280 6767
The old station buffet near the DART station has been renovated as an excellent fish restaurant. Great views from the bar while you enjoy a pre-dinner drink, and dishes such as deep-fried hake in a tortilla crust. $$

The Buttergate Restaurant
Millmount, Drogheda
Tel: 041-983 4759
In the grounds of Millmount on the outskirts of town, the Buttergate has wonderful views back over Drogheda and along the River Boyne. The food is a match for the views, with seafood naturally a good choice, but there is a range of other options, from steak to vegetarian. $$

Caviston's Seafood Restaurant
59 Glasthule Road,
Sandycove, Dún Laoghaire
Tel: 01-280 9120
Busy and unpretentious little seafood restaurant that delivers the best fresh fish, lunchtime (Tues–Sat) only, with sittings at noon, 1.30pm and 3pm. Terrific food store next door, with meats, oils, spices and other tempting items alongside the fish and shellfish. $$

King Sitric
East Pier, Howth
Tel: 01-832 5235
Old Dublin favourite in a 150-year-old harbour-master's building, which many people feel is worth taking the DART or driving out to Howth to visit. Local fish from a harbour overlooked by many of the tables. The signature Howth fish ragout combines the best of the day's catch. Fresh crab and lobster, too, from the owner's lobster pots out in the bay. Plenty of meat dishes as well and a good wine list. $$$

Poppie's
The Square, Enniskerry
Tel: 01-282 8869
If you are on a driving tour of the Wicklow Mountains, this is a great place to stop off for either breakfast, lunch, coffee, a snack or an early evening meal. There are lots of filling home-made dishes, such as quiches and casseroles, and the delicious desserts will tempt even the most resolute weight-watcher. $

Wicklow Heather Restaurant
Laragh, near Glendalough
Tel: 0404-45157
A pleasant but ordinary exterior belies the extraordinarily good food on offer, including salmon, venison and pork dishes cooked with fresh local products, as well as flair and imagination. Friendly service, open daily 8am–9pm, and well worth a visit. $$

Left: Bad Ass Café

leisure activities

Above: the Temple Bar area is at the hub of Dublin's nightlife

NIGHTLIFE

Dublin has so much nightlife that it could export half and still have a surfeit. In fact, this is exactly what happens – there are Irish pubs everywhere from Kuala Lumpur to Abu Dhabi. A lot of the city's nightlife focuses on the Temple Bar district, which is swamped by local youngsters and tourists alike. But the Temple Bar is full of culture, too, and in summer there is a programme of free outdoor films, concerts and other performances in Meeting House Square. Other options include organised Irish nights with traditional music and dancing, and the good old-fashioned Irish pub. These pubs buzz with talk as locals enjoy that particular Irish good time known as the *craic*.

Trendy Dubliners have discovered the joys of the cocktail bar, where they can meet in more sophisticated surroundings. Some of the newer hotels – the Clarence, the Morgan, the Fitzwilliam, the Morrison – are meeting precisely this market, if you want a business meeting or smarter rendezvous.

The Craic

The *craic* can't be defined, but can only be experienced, and if you don't know to begin with, you'll certainly know what it is after a few days in Dublin. It's a good time, sure, but it's more than a good time. It will definitely involve conversation, probably drink, there could be music, but it's more to do with the company and the atmosphere. 'It was good *craic*' can cover a night at the pub, a meal, a party, having a few friends home, maybe even just going for a stroll with your pals. It could even describe your whole visit to Dublin, and probably will.

Bars and Pubs

Pubs are one of Dublin's best features. Many are on the tourist trail, but none the worse for that, and there are still plenty (some included in the list below) that the locals keep for themselves. Even if you don't want a drink, look in the historic pubs to admire the elegant surroundings. Most open mid-morning, or noon, and stay open till late at night. Some may close for a 'holy hour', or short break in the afternoon. The following list only scratches the surface.

The Brazen Head
20 Lower Bridge Street
Tel: 01-679 5186
This pub, which claims to be the oldest in Dublin, if not Europe, is on a site close to the Liffey where there has been a tavern since 1198. Lovely cobbled courtyard, good food, and the place where rebels such as Wolfe Tone and Robert Emmet once drank.

David Byrne's
21 Duke Street
Tel: 01-677 5217
Legendary watering hole mentioned in

bars and pubs

nightlife

Ulysses, which attracts Joyce fans on Bloomsday *(see Calendar of Events, page 28)*. Michael Collins, and many a literary figure, drank here. It has been modernised but retains its character.

Doheny and Nesbitt
5 Lower Baggot Street
Tel: 01-676 2945
Popular with the politicians and journalists who work nearby. The atmospheric snugs (booths ideal for a small group of friends) downstairs are usually full but there is a more modern bar upstairs.

The Duke
9 Duke Street
Tel: 01-679 9553
James Joyce and Brendan Behan are just two of the literary lions to have drunk here. The Duke opened in 1822 and has kept its Victorian exterior, created during 1890s renovations. Its warren of rooms, upstairs and down, including an Oyster Bar, are usually packed, seven days a week.

The Long Hall
51 South Great George's Street
Tel: 01-475 1590
The Long Hall features a wood-and-glass Victorian interior and a hand-carved bar that is said to be the longest in Dublin. A small wooden arch separates the front bar from the rear. Engravings and mosaics enhance the down-to-earth atmosphere.

McDaid's
3 Harry Street
Tel: 01-679 4395
Originally the city morgue, McDaid's became the haunt of literary figures such as Brendan Behan and J.P. Donleavy, but it has kept up with the times and now attracts a mix of youngsters, traditionalists and curious visitors.

J. Mulligan
8 Poolbeg Street
Tel: 01-677 5582
Mulligan's is so ordinary and unfashionable that it has become deeply fashionable. No fancy decor, no laid-on Irish music and it's packed every night. Famous past visitors include President John F. Kennedy and Bing Crosby.

Neary's
1 Chatham Street
Tel: 01-677 7371
An Edwardian pub close to Grafton Street and the Gaiety Theatre, it attracts thespian types and shoppers alike. Traditional interior.

O'Donoghue's
15 Merrion Row
Tel: 01-661 4303
An old-time favourite where you're likely to hear music, either organised or impromptu. This is the pub that helped launch The Dubliners on their musical career.

The Old Stand
37 Exchequer Street
Tel: 01-677 7220
This well-run pub has always been popular with rugby fans. Bar food served daily from noon–9pm.

The Oliver St John Gogarty
58–59 Fleet Street
Tel: 01-671 1822
There is music every night till late in this popular Temple Bar pub/restaurant, with Sunday lunchtime and Saturday afternoon sessions too.

O'Neill's
2 Suffolk Street
Tel: 01-679 3656
Opposite the Tourist Information Centre, with a huge clock face marking the exterior, O'Neill's is frequented by tourists, students from nearby Trinity, and Dubliners meet-

Right: enjoying a brew is part of the fabric of Dublin life

leisure activities

ing in a network of rooms both large and small. Renowned for a lunchtime carvery.

The Palace
21 Fleet Street
Tel: 01-677 9290
The walls of The Palace tell the story of Dublin through posters, paintings, cartoons and the like. Close to the offices of *The Irish Times*, it has always attracted journalists recounting unpublishable Dublin tales.

Porterhouse Brewing Company
16-18 Parliament Street
Tel: 01-679 8847
The city's first micro-brewery, it won a 'Pub of the Year' award in 1998 for its 10 home-brewed beers, superior bar food and all-round convivial atmosphere.

Ryan's
28 Parkgate Street
Tel: 01-677 6097
A gem that's well worth visiting if you go to Phoenix Park. Its brass fittings, mirrors, mahogany bar and snugs all help preserve an old-fashioned ambience. Food is served 12.30–2.30pm and 5–9pm, and from 6–10.30pm in the separate restaurant.

The Stag's Head
1 Dame Court
Tel: 01-679 3701
A great Dublin pub, whose authentic local character is protected by its discreet location. Stags' heads do indeed adorn the walls, and the marble, mirrors and skylights make for a delightful drinking venue.

Cinemas
Dublin has several big-screen cinemas and for art-house, cult and independent movies the Irish Film Centre *(see page 40)*. The Screen, D'Olier Street, has three screens and a varied programme from blockbuster to foreign-language. The five-screen Savoy on O'Connell Street is the place to catch current releases. There are nine screens at the Parnell Centre, Parnell Street, but the biggest multiplex is the 12-screen UCI out of town to the northwest at the Blanchardstown Centre.

Comedy
The Comedy Cellar
23 Wicklow Street
Tel: 01-677 9250
Small and invariably full, so arrive early and be prepared for no-holds-barred routines.

The Ha'penny Bridge Inn
Wellington Quay
Tel: 086-815 6987
Comedy nights, along with some music and drama, every Tuesday from 9.30pm (doors open 9pm).

Murphy's Laughter Lounge
O'Connell Bridge (north side)
Tel: 800-COMEDY
A more professional approach to the burgeoning comedy scene, with performances from local and visiting comedians, Thur–Sat from 9pm (doors open 8pm).

Irish Nights
Arlington Hotel
Bachelors Walk
Tel: 01-804 9100
Free music and dancing every night from about 9pm in the hotel's vast Knightsbridge Bar, which also serves bar food. An excellent night out but good tables are in demand so arrive early or book in advance.

Above: stained glass
Left: enjoy the *craic*

theatres

nightlife

Jury's Irish Cabaret
Pembroke Road, Ballsbridge
Tel: 01-660 5000
Expensive and corny but a fun mix of comedy, music and dance, catering mainly to visiting groups.

Music and Nightclubs

Gaiety Theatre
South King Street
Tel: 01-679 5622
DJs and live music from salsa to soul and swing. Fri and Sat noon–4am in the Late Night Club.

HQ at the Hall of Fame
57 Middle Abbey Street
Tel: 01-878 3345
Intimate venue that attracts older audiences with classic rock and pop.

The Mean Fiddler
26 Wexford Street
Tel: 01-475 8555
This Dublin offshoot of the London original is the perfect small music venue, attracting known and unknown acts alike.

The Music Centre
Curved Street
Tel: 01-679 0533
Mostly for teenyboppers but this small venue does spin discs other than the bland 'boy band' guff.

PoD
Old Harcourt Street Train Station
Harcourt Street
Tel: 01-478 0225
Long-established clubbing venue, the Place of Dance (Wed–Sun till late, Wed for students, Fri gay night) is one of the best clubs in the city.

Switch
Eustace Street
Tel: 01-670 7655
Beneath the Riverhouse Hotel in Temple Bar, dancers are blasted by powerhouse music in this popular nightclub, featuring techno and other modern music.

Whelan's
25 Wexford Street
Tel: 01-478 0766
One of the city's best smaller venues for local and international acts, so check who's playing.

Theatres

Abbey Theatre
Lower Abbey Street
Tel: 01-878 7222
Ireland's premier stage for new talents and old favourites such as Synge and Wilde. The basement Peacock Theatre showcases new Irish talent.

Gaiety Theatre
South King Street
Tel: 01-677 1717
The place for pantomimes in winter, musicals all year, and good, wholesome, family entertainment.

Gate Theatre
Cavendish Row
Tel: 01-874 4045
Premieres of new Irish drama and works by 20th-century dramatists such as Harold Pinter and Noël Coward.

Olympia Theatre
72 Dame Street
Tel: 01-677 7744
Atmospheric Victorian theatre featuring Irish singers such as Mary Coughlan plus international acts.

Above: toe-tapping Irish dancer

CALENDAR OF EVENTS

Contact the Dublin Tourism Centre or the Irish Tourist Board for details of the many annual events, the dates of which change every year.

January–March

The **Six Nations rugby championships** pit Ireland against England, Scotland, Wales, France and Italy. Ireland's home games usually take place at Dublin's Lansdowne Road stadium (tel: 01-668 4601).

National Hunt meeting at Leopardstown.

Opening of **Point-to-Point** season. Races

are run at different venues every Sunday over unfenced courses.

Aer Lingus Young Scientists Exhibition, RDS Showgrounds, Ballsbridge.

February

Irish Motor Show, RDS, Ballsbridge.

March

The **Dublin Film Festival** of Irish and international films, plus talks and other events, takes place at cinemas throughout the city in March or April. Book ahead if you can, especially for talks by visiting stars and directors. It's a great showcase for Irish cinema, too (tel: 01-679 2937).

Above: St Patrick's Day celebrations
Right: Bloomsday aficionados

St Patrick's Day. On the days either side of the 17th, Dublin hosts all kinds of cultural and sporting events, from bands on street corners to aerial displays, all climaxing in a huge street parade followed by fireworks (tel: 01-676 3208).

During the **Temple Bar Fleadh** music festival (part of the St Patrick's Day festivities), the streets are even more packed than usual, with all kinds of music to be heard on the nearest weekend to the 17th.

April

The **Feis Ceoil** is an 11-day classical music festival that takes place at the RDS Showgrounds in Ballsbridge (tel: 01-676 7365) along with various other venues.

Handel's Messiah. On the 13th, the anniversary of the work's première in 1742, a commemorative concert takes place on the site of the Musick Hall, Fishamble Street.

Easter sees the **Opera Ireland Spring Season** at the Gaiety Theatre (tel: 01-677 1717).

Easter Monday brings the **Irish Grand National** (steeplechase) at Fairyhouse.

May

The **Wicklow Gardens Festival** runs till mid-July, with private gardens, including those at country houses such as Russborough House, opened to the public. Call 0404-66058 for details.

June

The **Festival of Music in Great Irish Houses** takes place over several days and brings classical musicians of international renown to Dublin and the neighbouring counties of Wicklow and Kildare, to perform in some of the country's finest Georgian and classical mansions (tel: 01-278 1528).

Music in the Parks usually starts in June and runs throughout the summer. Dublin Corporation funds a range of free concerts, including jazz, brass bands and swing, in parks throughout the city (tel: 01-672 3388).

Bloomsday. 16 June 1904 was the date on which James Joyce's novel *Ulysses*, with its hero Leopold Bloom, was set. In the preceding week, walks, talks, concerts, films, meals and get-togethers throughout the city lead up to the 16th, when suitably costumed

calendar of events

characters stroll through the streets. For further details contact the James Joyce Centre (tel: 01-878 8547).

July

The **Guinness Blues Festival** turns Temple Bar into Chicago for a few days in late July. Events include a free concert at College Green and visiting musicians in pubs and clubs (tel: 01-497 0381).

Trinity College Summer Schools offer visitors the chance to be students, staying on the Trinity College campus. There are other summer schools in and around Dublin, many focusing on Irish matters: contact your nearest Irish Tourist Board for details. There is also a **James Joyce Summer School**, with lectures and seminars, held at Newman House, St Stephen's Green, where Joyce studied (tel: 01-878 8547).

August

The **Bray International Festival of Music and Dance**. Irish music and dance at a three-day event in early Aug (tel: 01-286 0080).
Dublin Horse Show. Showjumping, dressage and other displays in the biggest event of its kind in Ireland. Visitors come from around the world to the RDS Showgrounds in Ballsbridge (tel: 01-668 0866).
The **Temple Bar Blues Festival** sees a weekend of music on the streets.
Summer Music Festival. Eclectic collection of music and drama on St Stephen's Green in the last two weeks of August.

September

The **All-Ireland Hurling and Gaelic Football finals**. These two major sporting events take place at Croke Park (tel: 01-836 3222). The **Irish Antique Dealers' Fair** is held at the RDS Showgrounds in Ballsbridge (tel: 061-396409).
For three weeks starting in late September, the **Dublin Fringe Festival** covers most art forms in an attempt to rival the rather more famous Edinburgh Fringe Festival (tel: 01-872 9016).

October

Dublin Theatre Festival. Premières of new works by Irish and foreign writers are staged at theatres throughout the city for two weeks in mid-October. The festival has been going since 1957 and is very popular, so book ahead (tel: 01-677 8439).
The **Dublin City Marathon** is run on the last Monday in October (tel: 01-676 4647). The **Oscar Wilde Autumn School** is held in Bray (tel: 01-286 5245).

December

The **Dublin Grand Opera** winter season opens in early December at the Gaiety Theatre (tel: 01-677 1717).
The **National Crafts Fair of Ireland** is held just before Christmas at the RDS Showgrounds in Ballsbridge (tel: 01-867 1517). The **Christmas Horse Racing Festival**, on 26–29th at the Leopardstown Race Course.

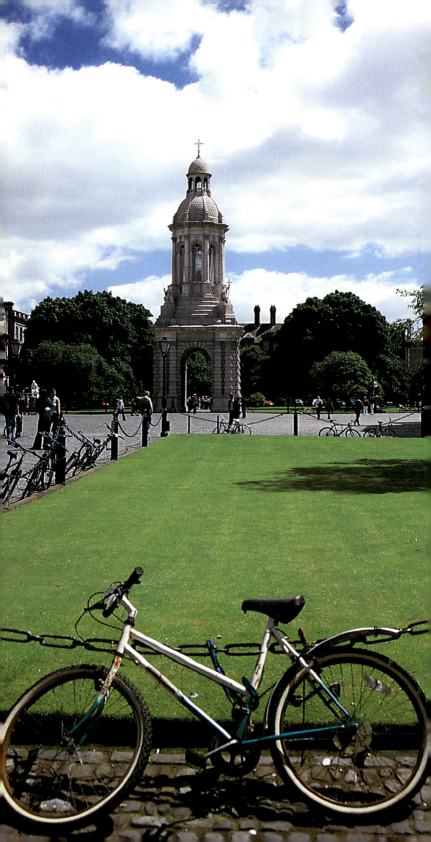

Practical Information

GETTING THERE

Arriving by Air
Dublin International Airport (tel: 01-704 2222) is 7½ miles (12 km) north of the centre, to which there are several transport links. The cheapest way to travel is on the Airlink bus (Mon–Sat 6.40am–11pm, Sun 7am–11pm) which runs between the airport and the main city bus station, Busáras, a few minutes' walk from O'Connell Bridge. The Aircoach bus, costing slightly more, makes several stops in the city, including O'Connell Street, Grafton Street and St Stephen's Green and runs every 15 minutes (5.30am–11.30pm). The journey should take approximately 30 minutes but can be much longer during busy periods as Dublin's streets cannot cope with the volume of modern-day traffic.

In addition, numerous local bus services also stop directly outside the terminal building. Tickets cost about a third of the price of coach tickets but journey times are much longer because of the large number of stops. Numbers and routes are displayed on the bus stops directly outside the terminal building. Be aware that you will need to present the exact change to the bus driver (there are change machines near the bus stops). No. 41 drops passengers off at Abbey Street Lower and picks up at Eden Quay, both near O'Connell Bridge.

Taxis are more expensive and convenient but are not necessarily quicker than coaches.

Most major car hire companies have booths at the airport, where there is also a good tourist information office and ATMs.

Leaving by Air
There is a departure tax, which is included in the price of a plane ticket.

Arriving by Sea
Dublin has two ferry terminals. Dublin Port is 2 miles (3 km) east of the city centre and linked to the Busáras bus station by the No. 53 bus, which is scheduled to meet arrivals. The port at Dún Laoghaire (pronounced Dunleary) is 8 miles (13 km) southeast of the centre and has its own DART (Dublin Area Rapid Transit) train station. The journey takes about 20 minutes. Dún Laoghaire has tourist information, money exchange and ATM facilities.

Arriving by Train
If travelling to Dublin from elsewhere in Eire, or from Northern Ireland, there are two main stations. The central Connolly Station, which is on the DART line, is the busier; Heuston Station is just west of the city centre, and linked to it by the No. 90 bus.

TRAVEL ESSENTIALS

Visas and Passports
Passport holders from Europe, North America and many other places do not need a visa to enter Ireland.

UK nationals who were born in Great Britain or Northern Ireland do not require a passport, but it is useful to take one as a form of identification.

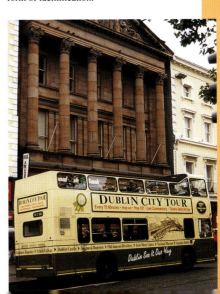

Left: bicycles at Trinity College
Right: one way to see the sights

Vaccinations
No vaccinations are needed to enter Ireland.

Customs
Citizens of EU countries have no restrictions on tax-paid goods brought into Ireland from other EU countries provided they are for their own personal consumption. Citizens of most other countries, including the US and Canada, can bring in 200 cigarettes, 1 litre of spirits, 2 litres of wine and other goods to the value of £34. US and Canadian citizens can export goods to the value of $400 and $300 respectively, plus a tobacco allowance of 200 cigarettes, 100 cigarillos, 50 cigars or 250g of tobacco. Citizens of other countries should check.

Firearms, explosives, drugs, obscene material, all meats and meat products and all plants and plant products, including seeds, are illegal.

Climate and When to Go
The summer months (July–September) are best, but the weather in Ireland is notoriously unpredictable and it is not unusual to experience all four seasons in one day. If you don't like the weather, one saying goes, just wait 10 minutes and it will change. The climate is generally mild. Summer temperatures can reach 80°F (27°C) and occasionally beyond; in winter the temperature seldom drops below freezing. Winters tend to see rain rather than snow, but it can rain at any time of year, so always take waterproofs and an umbrella.

Electricity
220V AC; plugs have three square pin Most hotels have 110V shaving sockets.

Time Difference
Dublin is on Greenwich Mean Time. As i Britain, clocks are put forward one hour i spring and back one hour in autumn. Ignor ing this adjustment, Dublin is five hour ahead of New York, nine hours ahead of Lo Angeles and 10 hours behind Sydney.

GETTING ACQUAINTED

Religion
Like the country as a whole, Dublin i predominantly Roman Catholic, although there is a more sizeable Protestant popula tion here than elsewhere in the country Catholicism is not the official religion although the Church does wield considerable – if slowly waning – power.

How Not to Offend
Religion is a less touchy subject here than it is in Northern Ireland, but beliefs are still to be respected. Dubliners are naturally friendly and talkative, so don't be offhand if a complete stranger strikes up a conversation with you. Don't test the local tolerance by trying to tell Irish jokes.

Language
English is spoken throughout Dublin and you will rarely hear anyone speak Irish, despite the fact that it is taught in every school. Irish has undergone a revival in recent years – you will see it used alongside English on road signs, official documents, public transport and the like.

Money Matters
Ireland has signed up to the new European Common Currency, the Euro. Since 1 January 2002, Euro notes and coins have been used alongside the existing currency; the Irish pound, the punt, is due to be withdrawn in July 2002. Till then, 'pounds' refers to the punt; 'pounds sterling' to British pounds.

Traveller's cheques and foreign currency can be exchanged throughout Dublin. In addition to numerous *bureaux de change*,

Left: the welcome is warm even when the weather is wet

getting around

...ere are banks on every high street. There ...e also countless ATM machines for cash ...ithdrawals, with all the major cards cov-...ed. Credit cards can be used widely, par-...cularly in the larger stores.

Tipping

A tip of about 10–15 percent is usual in restaurants and taxis, though some restaurants include an 'optional' service charge on the bill so a tip is not neccesary. Porters and tour guides should also be tipped according to the work they have done, but it is not customary to tip in cinemas, theatres or bars. If you have had a pleasant time over a few drinks in a bar, you might tell the barman to 'have one for yourself' when you buy the next round.

GETTING AROUND

Domestic Flights

Ireland has several domestic airports, at Cork, Donegal, Galway, Kerry, Knock, Sligo and Waterford. They are served by a number of airline companies, including Aer Lingus and Ryanair. Flying is by far the quickest way to get around Ireland if you plan on moving on from Dublin. Internal fares are relatively cheap.

Taxis

Taxis are plentiful but are not normally hailed on the street. Instead, they wait for fares at numerous taxi ranks, near hotels, train and bus stations, and central spots such as College Green (outside Trinity College) and O'Connell Street. You can also telephone for a taxi: there are numerous companies listed in the telephone directory.

Fares are fixed by law and are metered. Taxis are not expensive except when they get caught up in the busy Dublin traffic, so try to avoid using them in peak periods (although that has come to incorporate much of the day). There is an additional charge for taxis from the airport.

Trains

Dublin's city train service is called the DART (Dublin Area Rapid Transit), and it usually lives up to its name. Services are generally punctual and quick, and it is a cheap and convenient way to get around, although there are only a limited number of stations in the city centre. The service also extends north to places such as Howth and Malahide, and south to Dún Laoghaire, Dalkey and Bray.

practical information

The DART operates from Mon–Sat 7am–11.30pm and Sun 9.30am–11.30pm. Timetables and maps are available at main stations and tourist information offices. There is a minimum fare for a singe journey, depending on the distance; day passes, family cards and four-day passes cover both the DART and buses. For information, contact DART (tel: 01-703 3504).

Buses

The Dublin Bus company operates services throughout the city. Buses are inexpensive but can be crowded and slow. They can be a convenient way of getting to attractions beyond the city centre that are not on the DART, such as Phoenix Park or the National Botanical Gardens.

Most services run about every 15 minutes, 6am–11.30pm, although there are also suburban night buses till 3am on Thursday, Friday and Saturday nights. Bus stops cluster in places such as O'Connell Street, Eden Quay and Aston Quay. Stops give the numbers and routes of the buses. Fares vary according to the number of stops travelled: ask the driver when you board. Have plenty of coins ready as you often need to have the exact fare. For information call Dublin Bus (tel: 01-873 4222).

Car Hire

You do not need a car to make the most of a trip to Dublin. Conversely, a hired car is the ideal way in which to escape the city centre and be out in the Irish countryside in 30 minutes. All the major car hire companies have offices, most in the city centre and at the airport. The best of the local companies include Argus (tel: 01-490 4444) and Dan Dooley (01-677 2723).

To rent a car you must have held a full clean driver's licence for at least two years and normally be aged between 23 and 70. Some companies are more flexible, but you must be at least 21. Car hire can be expensive, with an additional charge if you wish to travel into Northern Ireland. Most cars are manual, not automatic. Road signs in Ireland are very poor, so be sure to take a good road map and be prepared to ask locals for directions. Fortunately, most people are extremely helpful.

HOURS AND HOLIDAYS

Business Hours

General office hours are Mon–Fri 9am–5pm. Shops stay open a little later, especially in central Dublin. On Thursday they stay open till 8 or 9pm. Shops are open on Saturday and some in the city centre on Sunday too. There are also several 24-hour general stores.

Banks

Usual hours are Mon–Fri 10am–4pm (until 5pm on Thursday).

Post Office

Most post offices are open Mon–Fri 9am–5.30pm, and some Sat 9am–1pm. The GPO on O'Connell Street *(see pages 41–42)* is open Mon–Sat 8am–8pm, Sun and holidays 10am–6.30pm for limited transactions such as selling stamps and exchanging money.

Public Holidays

New Year's Day
St Patrick's Day (17 March)
Good Friday
Easter Monday
May Day (1 May)
June Holiday (first Monday in June)
August Holiday (first Monday in August)
October Holiday (first Monday in October)
Christmas Day
St Stephen's Day/Boxing Day
If St Patrick's Day, May Day or Boxing Day fall on a Saturday or Sunday, the holiday is taken on the Monday.

Left: green postboxes for an Emerald Isle

accommodation

ACCOMMODATION

The accommodation space in Dublin hasn't kept pace with the boom in the city's popularity, so booking ahead is advisable. New hotels have been shooting up in recent years, with more being built all the time, but you should plan ahead, especially if you want to stay in the city centre or in a particular area. If you are going to stay outside the centre, try and find accommodation near a DART station, a quick and economic way to get to the centre of a city with serious traffic problems.

Bear in mind that there is an even bigger shortage of accommodation in the cheaper price brackets. There are many fine hotels right in the city, but they do tend to be more expensive; the newer hotels also are mostly aimed at the upper end of the market.

But you should find somewhere at the price you can afford, provided you give yourself enough time. If you arrive and are stuck, the Dublin Tourism Centre on Suffolk Street has an accommodation booking service at a modest price, whether you are looking for hostels or Hiltons *(see page 91)*.

The price ranges given below are per person sharing an ordinary double room. Breakfast is normally included in the price.

Luxury (95 Euros)

The Clarence
5–8 Wellington Quay, Dublin 2
Tel: 01-407 0800
Fax: 01-407 0820
Website: www.theclarence.ie
Email: reservations@theclarence.ie
Looking out on the Liffey in trendy Temple Bar, the Clarence combines minimalist decor with maximum luxury. It attracts visiting movie and rock stars – the rock group U2 invested in its 1996 makeover.

The Four Seasons
Simmonscourt Road, Ballsbridge, Dublin 4
Tel: 01-665 4000
Fax: 01-665 4099
Website: www.fourseasons.com/dublin
E-mail: dublin@fourseasons.com
New international hotel located to the south of the city centre, with 259 guest rooms, a health club, indoor pool and other amenities, all set within the historic Royal Dublin Society Showgrounds.

The Shelbourne
27 St Stephen's Green, Dublin 2
Tel: 01-663 4500
Fax: 01-661 6006
Website: www.shelbourne.ie
E-mail: shelbourneinfo@forte-hotels.com
Ireland's constitution was signed here in 1921, almost 100 years after this distinguished hotel was first built. It is favoured by visiting politicians, film stars and other celebrities, who love its discreet charm, period furniture, modern luxuries and perfect location.

Expensive (70–95 Euros)

Brooks Hotel
59–62 Drury Street, Dublin 2
Tel: 01-670 4000
Fax: 01-670 4455
Email: reservations@brookshotel.ie

Top: dining room at The Clarence
Right: The Shelbourne Hotel

practical information

practical information

Boutique-style hotel with 75 smart rooms in a central location and offering its own secure parking, which is always a bonus in Dublin.

The Gresham
O'Connell Street, Dublin 1
Tel: 01-874 6881
Fax: 01-878 7175
Email: gresham@indigo.ie
Large and venerable 4-star hotel, with 288 bedrooms and six suites. Recently refurbished, and always one of the first choices for the comfort-seeking visitor.

The Merrion
Upper Merrion Street, Dublin 2
Tel: 01-603 0600
Fax: 01-603 0700
Website: www.merrionhotel.com
Email: info@merrionhotel.com
Four splendid Georgian houses just off Merrion Square were converted in 1997 into a stylish, modern hotel that retains its Georgian features. Its sumptuous swimming pool and spa are just two features that have helped it win several Hotel of the Year awards.

Moderate (50–70 Euros)
The Alexander Hotel
Merrion Square, Dublin 2
Tel: 01-607 3700
Fax: 01-661 5663
Website: www.alexanderhotel.ie
Email: alexanderres@ocallaghanhotels.ie
The Alexander's 100 colourful, modern rooms all have modems, voice mail and international TV as standard. Executi suites, gym, conference facilities.

Butlers Town House
44 Lansdowne Road, Ballsbridge, Dublin
Tel: 01-667 4022
Fax: 01-667 3960
This 1996 restoration of a Victorian terrac house is an affordable, stylish option in t southern suburb of Ballsbridge..

The Davenport Hotel
Merrion Square, Dublin 2
Tel: 01-607 3500
Fax: 01-661 5663
Website: www.davenporthotel.ie
Email: davenportres@ocallaghanhotels.i
The Davenport's magnificent 1863 frontag has been lovingly restored. Inside there ar 120 rooms and suites, conference suites, gym and a restaurant.

Jurys Inn Custom House
Custom House Quay, Dublin 1
Tel: 01-607 5000
Fax: 01-829 0400
Email: customhouse_inn@jurysdoyle.com
A branch of Jury's Irish hotel empire, se right by the Liffey, appeals to visitors wh want basic comforts rather than luxury. Sim ilar hotels are in Christchurch Place, Balls bridge, Drumcondra and elsewhere.

Inexpensive (30–40 Euros)
The Arlington Hotel
23–25 Bachelors Walk
O'Connell Bridge, Dublin 1
Tel: 01-804 9100
Fax: 01-804 9112
Website: www.arlington.ie
Email: arlington@tinet.ie
Three-star hotel with medieval-style public rooms contrasting with modern bedrooms and suites. Front rooms overlook the Liffey. Underground car park.

Ashling Hotel Best Western
Parkgate Street, Dublin 8
Tel: 01-677 2324
Fax: 01-679 3783
Website: www.ashlinghotel.ie
Email: info:@ashlinghotel.ie
Situated a short walk from the city centre

Above: the Davenport Hotel's 19th-century facade

accommodation

convenient for anyone arriving at [H]uston Station, the Ashling Hotel offers [aff]ordable and comfortable rooms in typi[ca]l Best Western style.

[Ca]ulfields Hotel
[17]–19 Dorset Street, Dublin 1
[Te]l: 01-878 1550/878 0643
[Fa]x: 01-878 1650
[Em]ail: caulfieldshotel@tinet.ie

[A] short walk north of the city centre, [Ca]ulfields has 20 homely, en-suite rooms, [a f]riendly welcome and a popular music bar [on] the ground floor.

[D]rury Court Hotel
[2]8–30 Lower Stephen's Street, Dublin 2
[Te]l: 01-475 1988
[F]ax: 01-478 5730
[E]mail: druryct@indigo.ir

[T]he Drury Court Hotel is a popular option [si]tuated in central Dublin, not far from St [S]tephen's Green and within easy walking [di]stance of most of the main attractions. [T]here are 32 large and comfortable rooms, [a]t a 3-star price level.

Budget (under 30 Euros)

Aberdeen Lodge
53–55 Park Avenue
Ailesbury Road, Dublin 4
Tel: 01-283 8155
Fax: 01-283 7877
Website: www.greenbook.ie/aberdeen
Email: aberdeen@iol.ie

Located in Ballsbridge (where many foreign embassies are located), this 20-room hotel is part of the Charming Hotels group, as is its near neighbour, the Merrion Hall (tel: 01-283 8155). Both establishments are intimate, elegant places, handy for the RDS Convention Centre and the DART train into central Dublin.

Maple Hotel
75 Lower Gardiner Street, Dublin 1
Tel: 01-874 0225
Fax: 01-874 5239

Conveniently situated between O'Connell Street and Connolly Station, this long-established family-run hotel has just 10 rooms, all en suite. Inexpensive prices, two-star comfort and private parking.

Trinity College Accommodation
Accommodation Office
West Chapel
Trinity College, Dublin 2
Tel: 01-608 1177
Fax: 01-671 1267
Website: http://www2.tcd.ie/Accomm
Email: Reservations@tcd.ie

From June to September, student rooms – some en-suite – and apartments provide cheap and simple accommodation in a stunning setting.

Hostels

The Independent Holiday Hostels of Ireland Association lists 18 hostels in the city, most of them in the central Dublin 1 and Dublin 2 districts. With about 2,000 beds in all, and prices ranging from roughly 7 Euros per night for the most basic room out of season, no budget traveller should have trouble finding somewhere to stay, but it is still advisable to plan ahead.

For hostel details, contact the IHHI, 57 Lower Gardiner Street, Dublin 1 (tel: 01-836 4700; fax: 01-836 4710; email: ihh@iol.ie; website: www.hostels-ireland.com).

B&Bs outside Dublin

Hounslow House
Fore
Castlepollard
Co. Westmeath
Tel: 044-61144
Fax: 044-61847
Email: Eithne_Healy_Hounslow@MailAndNews.com

Wonderful 200-year-old farmhouse on the edge of the lovely little village of Fore *(see page 65)*. Bright, modern bedrooms. The owners are the epitome of Irish warmth and hospitality. Tea and home-baked scones on arrival. Closed in winter.

Glendale
Laragh
Glendalough
Co Wicklow
Tel: 0404-45410

Four en-suite rooms in a family-run, modern country house, just a few minutes from Laragh *(see page 60)*. Friendly welcome, spotless accommodation. Closed Dec–Jan.

practical information

Cloncarlin Farmhouse
Norney Road
Monastrevin
Co. Kildare
Tel: 045-525722

Six rooms in an 18th-century, family-run farmhouse on 180 acres (73 ha). Peace and quiet are guaranteed. The rooms are comfortable and old-fashioned, but with modern conveniences and a warm welcome. Closed Dec–Jan.

HEALTH AND EMERGENCIES

Hygiene and Health

There are no particular health concerns to take into account when visiting Dublin, although it is always advisable to take out health insurance in advance. EU citizens can claim free treatment by using form E111, available from post offices or social security offices before travelling, but citizens of non-EU countries will be expected to pay for any treatment administered.

There is a 24-hour accident and emergency department at Beaumont Hospital, Beaumont Road (tel: 01-837 7755), northeast of the centre on the way to the airport. In addition, there are A&E departments at St James's, 1 James Street (tel: 01-453 7941) and Mater Hospital, Eccles Street (tel: 01-803 2000). There are numerous pharmacies, with O'Connell's, 55 O'Connell Street Lower (tel: 01-873 0427) open daily till 10pm.

Theft or Loss of Belongings

Dublin is no more dangerous than any other city. It has its share of bag-snatching and pickpocketing, but you need to be careful rather than paranoid about it. Report any loss of belongings to the nearest police station: the police in Ireland are known as the Gardai. Call the main station on Harcourt Street, south of St Stephen's Green (tel: 01-475 5555) for details of your nearest station, or ring 999 or 112 in an emergency.

Emergency Services

For fire, police, ambulance, boat or coastal rescue services, dial 999 or 112 free from any telephone.

COMMUNICATION AND NEWS

Telephone

Many call boxes accept coins, credit cards or prepaid phone cards, which are available from newsagents, post offices and Telecom Éireann outlets. Many boxes also have a language assistance button. For international calls dial 00 before dialling the country code and number you require. Dial 11811 for directory enquiries in Ireland, and 11818 for international directory enquiries.

Newspapers and Magazines

Ireland has two national, daily, broadsheet newspapers, the *Irish Times* and the *Irish Independent*. Both also have Sunday editions, and there are four other Sunday newspapers. The *Evening Herald* appears on weekdays. British newspapers are widely available; larger newsagents stock other major European newspapers and magazines, and some from further afield. Try Eason's, 40 O'Connell Street Lower.

There are several listings magazines to keep you informed on what is going on in the city. *In Dublin* and the *Event Guide* both appear fortnightly, and the latter is free. Similar publications include *The List*, *The Slate* and *The Tourist Times*.

Television and Radio

The national broadcasting company is Radio Telefís Éirann, which has two networked channels in English, RTÉ1 and Network 2, and an Irish-language channel with English subtitles, Telefis Na Gaeilge. There is one independent channel, TV3, and Dublin can pick up the five British terrestrial channels. There are also numerous cable and satellite channels.

RTÉ has three radio channels: Radio 1 carries news, arts, talk shows and easy-listening music, 2FM broadcasts music for teenagers, and FM3 has classical music and minority-interest broadcasts. Dublin also has several independent stations.

Internet Cafés

It is difficult to walk any distance in Dublin these days without coming across a new internet café. Among the most central are

SPORT

Fishing
Sea-fishing excursions can be arranged in places such as Dalkey, Dún Laoghaire and Howth, all easily accessible on the DART from central Dublin. Dublin Tourism publishes a booklet giving information on fishing here and in lakes and rivers around the city. You can try trout fishing at the Glendalough and Annamoe Trout Fishery (tel: 0404-45470) about 20 miles (32 km) south of Dublin.

Gaelic Sports
The popularity of Gaelic football and hurling can be seen from the Sunday afternoon crowds that head out to the Croke Park Stadium (tel: 01-836 3222), where matches take place all year round.

Golf
The Celtic Tiger has had its effect on the sport of Tiger Woods. There are numerous championship courses in and around Dublin, most of which welcome non-members and charge reasonable green fees, especially during the week. The biggest course in the country is the Deer Park, Howth (tel: 01-832 2624), with five courses altogether. There is also an 18-hole course at the Dún Laoghaire Golf Club (tel: 01-280 1694).

In the countryside around Dublin, some of the best clubs are in Kildare, including the Kildare Country Club (tel: 01-627 3333) and the nearby Curragh Golf Club (tel: 045-441238). There are also numerous clubs in County Meath, including the scenic par-71 course at Ashbourne Golf club (tel: 01-835 2005) and a par-70 course at the Royal Tara Golf Club (tel: 046-25508).

Horse-racing
Dublin's Leopardstown race course is just south of the centre on Leopardstown Road in Foxrock (tel: 01-289 3607). Races take place all year round, usually at weekends.

Another of the country's major courses is the Curragh, east of Kildare. The country's major flat races are held here.

Horse-riding
There are several horse riding venues around Dublin: check with the Dublin Tourism Centre or local tourist information offices. There are several stables in County Meath, including the Kells Equestrian Centre (tel: 046-46998) and Rathe House (tel: 046-52376) in Kilmainham, which also offers archery, course fishing, clay pigeon shooting and other activities.

Rugby
Lansdowne Road (tel: 01-668 4601) in Ballsbridge is Ireland's national stadium. Home games in the Six Nations rugby championships are held here every year. The venue also hosts the clubs' all-Ireland finals. There are several club sides in Dublin: see the local press for details of fixtures over the winter rugby season.

Soccer
Association Football is very popular in Dublin – international matches are often played at Lansdowne Road. Dublin also has several teams in the premier division of the League of Ireland: see local press for fixture details in the Aug–May season.

Water Sports
If you don't mind sea water that remains chilly all year round, you can enjoy swimming and other water sports in and around Dublin. There are sandy beaches at Sutton and Malahide, both easily reached on the DART north of Dublin.

There are sailing clubs in Malahide, Howth, Clontarf and Dún Laoghaire, but you will usually need to be a member of a club

Right: horse-racing is an Irish passion

with reciprocal membership arrangements in order to participate. Contact the Irish Sailing Association (tel: 01-280 0239) for details.

To have a go at windsurfing or diving, head for Dalkey, where both can easily be arranged. There is also a windsurfing club at Dún Laoghaire.

ATTRACTIONS

Museum Passes

The city is not well-served by discount passes. Dublin Tourism offers a pass covering seven diverse attractions: the Dublin Writers' Museum, Dublin's Viking Adventure, the Fry Model Railway, the James Joyce Museum, Malahide Castle, Newbridge House and the Shaw Birthplace. A year pass covering a single admission to each attraction costs £15 for an adult.

The Heritage Card (adults £15) covers the six national parks and monuments that charge admission fees: Kilmainham Gaol, the Marino Casino, Phoenix Park Visitor Centre, Rathfarnham Castle, St Mary's Abbey and the Waterways Visitor Centre.

Tours and Walks

There are several excellent, themed walking tours in Dublin, including the Literary/Georgian Walk (tel: 01-496 0641), the excellent Literary Pub Crawl (tel: 01-670 5602), the Walk Macabre (tel: 087-677 1512), the Zozimus Ghostly Experience (tel: 01-661 8646), the Musical Pub Crawl (tel: 01-671 1822), Historical Walking Tours (tel: 01-878 0227) and the 1916 Rebellion Walking Tour (tel: 01-676 2493).

Several companies organise bus tours in and around Dublin and many of them include sites covered in the Excursions section of this book. Get up-to-date details from the Dublin Tourism Centre, which can also make bookings for you.

The city is served by a number of hop-on-hop off buses which run at 15-minute intervals and link many of the main attractions. Several services use the same bus stops, so you rarely need to wait more than a few minutes for a bus in high season. One ticket is valid for a full day, and it's a good way to get around if you want to fit in several attractions in one day.

Dublin Bike Tours (tel: 01-679 0899) offer a number of themed bicycle tours around the city, including a 'Dublin at Dawn' tour on Saturday.

FOR CHILDREN

Dublin Zoo (Mar–Oct Mon–Sat 9.30am–6pm, Sun 10.30am–6pm; Nov–Feb Mon–Sat 9.30–5pm, Sun 10.30am–5pm; admission fee) was founded in 1830 and is the third-oldest public zoo in the world. Like many zoos, it now gives the animals more space and more natural habitats. It concentrates on endangered species with a view to returning them to the wild, where possible. A new exhibit is the African Plains area, spread across 30 acres (12.5 ha), while the zoo's City Farm remains a perennial hands-on attraction for children.

The Ark (tel: 01-670 7788) on Eustace Street in Temple Bar is a cultural centre for children that puts on an extremely varied programme of events, including flamenco dancing, clock-making and book-making workshops, for children aged 3–14. Book ahead as numbers are limited.

Free family events also take place in Temple Bar's Meeting House Square every Sunday in summer (tel: 01-671 5717).

USEFUL INFORMATION

Tourist Information Offices

The main Dublin Tourism Centre (open July and Aug Mon–Sat 9am–6.30pm, Sun and holidays 10.30am–3pm; Sept–June Mon–

Left: one of many themed tours

further reading

at 9am–5.30pm) can be found near Trinity College in St Andrew's Church, Suffolk Street, Dublin 2 (for accommodation and ticket reservations only, tel: 01-605 7777; email: information@dublintourism.ie). It is comprehensively stocked with leaflets, books and souvenirs and provides many services such as booking accommodation, transport, tours and theatres. Assistants will point you in the right direction when you enter – take a ticket to join the numbered queueing system.

There is also a money exchange, telephones and car rental desks.

There are other offices at O'Connell Street, Baggot Street Bridge (tel: 01-284 4768), the airport arrivals hall (tel: 01-844 5387), the Dún Laoghaire ferry terminal (tel: 01-284 6361) and the Square, Tallaght, Dublin 24 (tel: 01-462 0671). The two largest offices at Suffolk Street and O'Connell Street do not have direct telephone information lines. Ring their number for information on the whole of Ireland (tel: 1850-230330) from within Ireland only.

For similar information on the County Wicklow area, contact Wicklow County Tourism (St Manntan's House, Kilmantin Hill, Wicklow Town, Co Wicklow, tel: 0404-66058, fax: 0404-66057; www.wicklow.ie; email: wctr@iol.ie

Irish Tourist Board Offices Abroad
Australia: 36 Carrington Street, 5th level, Sydney, NSW 2000 (tel: 02-9299 6177).
Canada: 160 Bloor St. E., Suite 1150, Toronto, Ontario M4W 1B9 (tel: 416-929 2777).
UK: 150 New Bond Street, London W1Y 0AQ (tel: 020-7493 3201).
USA: 345 Park Avenue, New York, NY 10154 (tel: 800-223 6470).

Embassies/Consulates in Dublin
Australia: Fitzwilton House, Wilton Terrace, Dublin 2 (tel: 01-676 1517).
Canada: 65–68 St Stephen's Green, Dublin 2 (tel: 01-478 1988).
UK: 29 Merrion Road, Dublin 4 (tel: 01-205 3700).
USA: 42 Elgin Road, Ballsbridge, Dublin 4 (tel: 01-668 8777).

FURTHER READING

Insight Guides
Insight Guide: Dublin and Surroundings (Apa Publications, 2001). A comprehensive look at Dublin, with stunning photographs, maps and practical tips.
Insight Guide: Ireland (Apa Publications, 2001). Full coverage of all the sights, plus background essays, great maps and photography and a comprehensive listings section.

Fiction
The ultimate Dublin book is James Joyce's *Ulysses*, a complicated and intertwining tale of 24 hours in the lives of various Dublin characters. For an easier read, try his short story collection, *Dubliners*.
J.P. Donleavy's *The Ginger Man* is a classic tale about a law student called Sebastian Dangerfield in postwar Dublin.
William Trevor and John McGahern are two of Ireland's finest late 20th-century novelists. *Mrs Eckdorf in O'Neill's Hotel* by Trevor and McGahern's *The Leavetaking* are both set in Dublin.
A Star Called Henry (Jonathan Cape) by Dublin's leading contemporary novelist, Roddy Doyle, portrays early 20th-century Dublin and the burgeoning Republican movement. His *Barrytown Trilogy* is a vivid picture of contemporary Dublin life.
Books not about Dublin but by writers associated with the city include *Dracula* by Bram Stoker, *Gulliver's Travels* by Jonathan Swift, *At Swim-Two-Birds* by Flann O'Brien and anything by Samuel Beckett and Oscar Wilde. Fine modern writers to look for include Dermot Bolger and Colm Tóibin.

Non-Fiction
Max Caulfield's *The Easter Rebellion* (Gill and McMillan) tells the story of that pivotal uprising.
Modern Ireland 1600–1972 by Roy Foster (Penguin) is the ultimate book on modern Irish history, but not for a casual read.
The Green Flag by Robert Kee (Penguin) is a journalist's account of the founding of modern Ireland.
Colm Tóibin's *The Irish Famine* (Profile) is a moving and detailed account of that troubled period.

practical information

INSIGHT
Pocket Guides

> The travel guides that replace a tour guide – now better than ever with more listings and a fresh new design

Insight Pocket Guides pioneered a new approach to guidebooks, introducing the concept of the authors as "local hosts" who would provide readers with personal recommendations, just as they would give honest advice to a friend who came to stay. They also included a full-size pull-out map. Now, to cope with the needs of the 21st century, new editions in this growing series are being given a new look to make them more practical to use, and restaurant and hotel listings have been greatly expanded.

👁 INSIGHT GUIDES

The world's largest collection of visual travel guides

Now in association with

ACKNOWLEDGEMENTS

Photography by	
78	**Bord Fáilte**
7T, 46, 49, 56T, 60T, 63, 64T/B	**Donna Dailey**
15T	**Mary Evans Picture Library**
12B, 13, 14	**National Gallery of Ireland**
11	**National Museum of Ireland**
1, 2/3, 5, 6T, 6B, 7B, 8/9, 10, 16B, 20, 21, 22, 23, 24, 25, 26T/B, 27, 28, 29T/B, 30, 31T/B, 33T/B, 34, 35, 36T/B, 37, 38, 40T/B, 42T/B, 43, 44, 47, 48T/B, 51, 52, 59, 60B, 61, 65, 66, 67, 68T/B, 69, 70, 71, 72, 74, 75, 76T/B, 77, 79, 80, 81, 82, 84, 85T/B, 86, 90, 92	**Richard T. Nowitz/Apa**
39, 50T/B, 55, 57, 61, 62T/B, 89	**Marcus Wilson Smith/Apa**
45T/B, 53, 54, 56B	**Geray Sweeney/Apa**
15B	**Topham Picturepoint**
12T	**Trinity College Dublin**
Cover	**Eye Ubiquitous**
Back cover	**Richard T. Nowitz**
Cartography	**Maria Donnelly**
	Berndtson and Berndtson Publications
Cover Design	**Tanvir Virdee**

© Apa Publications GmbH & Co. Verlag KG Singapore Branch, Singapore

INDEX

Abbey Theatre 44
accommodation 85–88
Act of Union, 1801 14, 17, 23, 44
Anglo-Irish Treaty (1921) 15, 17
Anglo-Normans 11, 12, 17, 32, 34
Áras an Uachtaráin (President's Residence) 48
Archibald's Castle 54
Ark, The 40
Ashtown Castle 48

Baily Lighthouse 57
Balscadden Bay 56
Bank of Ireland Arts Centre 23
Bank of Ireland 23
Beckett, Samuel 14, 22, 43
Behan, Brendan 14, 43
Belvedere College 44
Bewley's Oriental Café 25
Black Death (plague) 12, 17
Book of Kells 22, 64
Booterstown 53
Botanical Gardens 21
Boyne Valley 21, 63–65
Boyne, Battle of the 13, 17, 63
Bray Head 55
Bray 55
Brian Boru 11, 17, 46, 56
Brú na Bóinne (Newgrange) 63–64
Bully's Acre 46

Casino 50
Castle, Richard 26, 31, 42, 59, 60
Castlepollard 65
Castletown House 62
Catholic Association 17
Catholic Emancipation Act 14, 17
Catholics/Catholicism 12, 14, 17
Cavendish, Lord 14
Celts/Celtic artefacts 11, 17, 31, 63–64
Chester Beatty Library 33
Chester Beatty, Sir Alfred 33
children's attractions 90
Christ Church Cathedral 12, 34
City Hall 33
civil war, 1922 15, 17
Clarence Hotel 38

Clontarf 57
Clontarf, Battle of 11, 17, 46, 56
Collins, Michael 11, 15, 17, 32, 47, 50
County Kildare 17, 61–62
Croke Park 50
Cromwell, Oliver 12, 17, 59
Curragh 61
Custom House 44

Dáil Eireann (Irish Parliament) 15, 16, 31, 32
Dalkey Castle and Heritage Centre 54
Dalkey Island 55
Dalkey 54–55
Davy Byrne's pub 24
De Valera, Eamon 11, 15, 16, 25, 45, 50
Douglas Hyde Gallery, Trinity College 23
Dowth (Neolithic tomb) 64
Drogheda 63
Dublin Bay 21, 53, 57
Dublin Castle 12, 14, 17, 32–33
Dublin Civic Museum 27
Dublin Experience 23
Dublin Writers' Museum 43
Dublin Zoo 48
Dublin's Viking Adventure 34
Dublinia 34
Dún Laoghaire 53, 56

Easter Rising 15, 17, 26, 33, 45
Emmet, Robert 14, 17, 25, 37
Enniskerry 60

Fianna Fáil 16
Fitzwilliam Square 28, 29
Four Courts 36
Fry Model Railway, Malahide 57

GAA Museum 50
Gallery of Photography 40–41
Garden of Remembrance 42
Gate Theatre 42
General Post Office (GPO) 17, 41–42
Glasnevin Cemetery 49
Glasnevin 49

index

Glendalough 60
Glenmacnass Waterfall 60
Goat's Castle 54–55
Goldsmith, Oliver 22
Government Buildings 30
Grafton Street 21, 24
Grand Canal 51, 62
Great Famine 14, 17, 50
Great Sugar Loaf Mountain 59
Guinness Storehouse 37
Guinness, Arthur Edward 25, 38

Ha'penny Bridge 39
Hall-Walker, Colonel William 62
Handel, George Frideric 13, 17, 34, 36
Hill of Slane 64
Hill of Tara 65
Home Rule 14, 17
Hopkins, Gerard Manley 25
horse-racing 61, 89
Hot Press Irish Music Hall of Fame 41
Howth 56
Hugh Lane Municipal Gallery of Modern Art 43
Huguenot Cemetery 29

Irish Film Centre 40
Irish Free State 15, 17, 29, 32
Irish Museum of Modern Art 46
Irish National Stud 62
Irish Republican Army (IRA) 14, 27
Irish Republican Brotherhood 14
Ironside army 12, 59
Iveagh House and Gardens 25
Iveagh Market Hall 35
Iveagh, Lord 35

James II 13, 63
James Joyce Cultural Centre 44
James Joyce Museum, Sandycove 54
Joyce, James 14, 24, 25, 43, 55

Kells, County Meath 22, 64
Kildare 61
Killiney Bay 55
Kilmainham Gaol 17, 45
Kilmainham Gate 45
King's Inns 43
Knowth (Neolithic tomb) 64

Leinster House 31
Leinster, Duke of 31
Liffey, River 11, 21, 38
Long Hall 27
Long Room, Trinity College 23
Loughcrew Cairns 65
Loughcrew Gardens 65

Malahide Castle 57
Malahide 57–8
Malone, Molly, statue of 23–24
Mansion House 32
Marino 50
Market Arcade 27
Marsh's Library 35
Martello towers 54, 55
Maternity Hospital 42
McCormack, John 44, 62
McMurrough, Dermot, King of Leinster 11
Meeting House Square 40
Mellifont Abbey 63
Merchants' Arch 39
Merrion Square 13, 28
Millennium Bridge 39
Monasterboice 63
Monasterevin 62
Moore Street Market 42
Mother Redcap's Market 36
Mountjoy Square 28
Muiredach's Cross 63
Musick Hall 34

Naas 61
National Botanic Gardens 49
National Concert Hall 26
National Gallery 30
National Library 30
National Maritime Museum, Dún Laoghaire 53
National Museum 31, 47
National Museum at Collins Barracks 47
National Photographic Archive 41
National Sea-Life Centre, Bray 55
National Wax Museum 43
Natural History Museum 30
Newgrange tomb (Brú na Bóinne) 17, 63–64

index

Newman House 25
Newman, Cardinal John Henry 25

O'Brien, Flann 25
O'Carolan, Turlough 35
O'Casey, Sean 14, 44
O'Connell Monument 41
O'Connell Street 21
O'Connell, Daniel 11, 14, 28, 50
O'Neill's 27
Old Jameson Distillery 37
Old Library, Trinity College 22
Old Stand, The 27
Oldbridge 63
Oscar Wilde House 28

Papal Cross 48
Parnell Square 21, 28, 42
Parnell, Charles Stewart 11, 14, 42, 50
Pearse, Patrick 42
Phoenix Monument 48
Phoenix Park 14, 47–48
Pitt, William 13
Plunkett, Joseph 45
Powerscourt Centre 25
Powerscourt House and Gardens 13, 59
Powerscourt Townhouse 27
Powerscourt Waterfall 60
Protestants/Protestantism 12, 13
Punchestown 61

Rebellion of 1798 13, 23
RHA Gallagher Gallery 29
Robertstown 62
Royal Canal 51
Royal College of Surgeons 26
Royal Hibernian Way 25
Royal Hospital Kilmainham 47
Royal Irish Academy 32
Russborough House 13, 30, 60
Ryan's Pub 47

Sally Gap 60
Sandycove 54
Shaw, George Bernard 14, 51
Shelbourne Hotel 29, 64
Sinn Féin 15
Slane Abbey 64
Smithfield Market 37

South Great George's Street 27
sport 89–90
St Anne's Church 25, 32
St Audoen churches 36
St Audoen's Arch 36
St Augustine and St John, Church of 36
St Brigid's Cathedral, Kildare 61
St Catherine's Church 37
St Columba 22, 64
St Columba's Church 64
St Michans' Church 36
St Nicholas of Myra Church 35
St Patrick 12, 17, 34, 53, 64
St Patrick's Cathedral 12, 13, 17, 34
St Patrick's Tower 37
St Stephen's Green Shopping Centre 27
St Stephen's Green 13, 21, 25, 28
Stoker, Bram 14, 31, 32, 43
Swift, Jonathan 13, 22, 34, 35
Synge, J.M. 14, 44

Tailors' Hall 36
Talbot Botanical Gardens 59
Temple Bar Music Centre 40
Temple Bar Square 39–40
Temple Bar 38–41
Tone, Wolfe 11, 13, 25, 32, 53
tourist offices 27, 90–91
Trim 65
Trinity College 12, 21–22
Tullynally Castle 65

U2 16, 38
United Irishmen 13
University Church 25

Vikings 11, 12, 22, 31

Waterways Visitor Centre 51
Wellington's Column 48
West Cross 63
Wicklow Mountains 21, 59–61
Wicklow 60
Wilde, Oscar 14, 22, 28, 32
William of Orange 13, 17, 63
Wood Quay 34

Yeats, W.B. 14, 25, 28, 30, 44, 56